STUDY GUIDE

to accompany

LIFELONG HUMAN DEVELOPMENT

ALISON CLARKE-STEWART
MARION PERLMUTTER
SUSAN FRIEDMAN

PREPARED BY:
STEHHEN LEPOIE
WENDY L. KLIEWER

WILEY

JOHN WILEY & SONS
New York • Chichester • Brisbane • Toronto • Singapore

ISBN 0 471 63415 8
Printed in the United States of America

10 9 8 7 6 5 4 3 2 1

DEDICATION

This <u>Study Guide</u> is dedicated to Susan Friedman, a co-author of <u>Lifelong Human Development</u>, who died tragically during the preparation of this guide. Her creativity will be missed.

CONTENTS

Contents

How to use this guide

PART ONE: Introduction

Chapter 1   History and theories   1

               Chapter Summary   1
               Learning Objectives   2
               Key Terms   3
               Study Questions   7
               Self-Test   11
               Answers to the Self-Test   15

Chapter 2   Methods   17

               Chapter Summary   17
               Learning Objectives   19
               Key Terms   19
               Study Questions   23
               Self-Test   27
               Answers to the Self-Test   31

PART TWO: Foundations

Chapter 3   Heredity and Environment   33

               Chapter Summary   33
               Learning Objectives   34
               Key Terms   35
               Study Questions   38
               Self-Test   40
               Answers to the Self-Test   44

Chapter 4   Prenatal development and birth   45

               Chapter Summary   45
               Learning Objectives   47
               Key Terms   47
               Study Questions   52
               Self-Test   54
               Answers to the Self-Test   58

PART THREE: Infancy

    Chapter 5   Physical and perceptual development 59

                  Chapter Summary 59
                  Learning Objectives 60
                  Key Terms 61
                  Study Questions 64
                  Self-Test 67
                  Answers to the Self-Test 71

    Chapter 6   Cognitive development 73

                  Chapter Summary 73
                  Learning Objectives 75
                  Key Terms 75
                  Study Questions 77
                  Self-Test 80
                  Answers to the Self-Test 84

    Chapter 7   Social and emotional development .. 85

                  Chapter Summary 85
                  Learning Objectives 87
                  Key Terms 88
                  Study Questions 89
                  Self-Test 92
                  Answers to the Self-Test 96

PART FOUR: Early childhood

    Chapter 8   Physical development 97

                  Chapter Summary 97
                  Learning Objectives 98
                  Key Terms 99
                  Study Questions 100
                  Self-Test 103
                  Answers to the Self-Test 107

    Chapter 9   Cognitive development 109

                  Chapter Summary 109
                  Learning Objectives 111
                  Key Terms 112
                  Study Questions 113
                  Self-Test 117
                  Answers to the Self-Test 122

Chapter 10   Social and emotional development . 123

                Chapter Summary 123
                Learning Objectives 125
                Key Terms 126
                Study Questions 127
                Self-Test 131
                Answers to the Self-Test 135

PART FIVE: **Middle childhood**

Chapter 11   Physical development 137

                Chapter Summary 137
                Learning Objectives 138
                Key Terms 138
                Study Questions 139
                Self-Test 142
                Answers to the Self-Test 146

Chapter 12   Cognitive development 147

                Chapter Summary 147
                Learning Objectives 149
                Key Terms 150
                Study Questions 151
                Self-Test 155
                Answers to the Self-Test 160

Chapter 13   Social and emotional development . 161

                Chapter Summary 161
                Learning Objectives 163
                Key Terms 164
                Study Questions 164
                Self-Test 168
                Answers to the Self-Test 172

PART SIX: **Adolescence**

Chapter 14   Physical development 173

                Chapter Summary 173
                Learning Objectives 174
                Key Terms 175
                Study Questions 176
                Self-Test 180
                Answers to the Self-Test 185

Chapter 15   Cognitive development 187

                Chapter Summary 187
                Learning Objectives 188
                Key Terms 189
                Study Questions 190
                Self-Test 194
                Answers to the Self-Test 198

Chapter 16   Social and emotional development . 199

                Chapter Summary 199
                Learning Objectives 201
                Key Terms 202
                Study Questions 203
                Self-Test 208
                Answers to the Self-Test 213

PART SEVEN: Early and middle adulthood

Chapter 17   Physical development 215

                Chapter Summary 215
                Learning Objectives 216
                Key Terms 217
                Study Questions 218
                Self-Test 223
                Answers to the Self-Test 227

Chapter 18   Cognitive development 229

                Chapter Summary 229
                Learning Objectives 231
                Key Terms 232
                Study Questions 233
                Self-Test 238
                Answers to the Self-Test 242

Chapter 19   Social development 243

                Chapter Summary 243
                Learning Objectives 246
                Key Terms 247
                Study Questions 248
                Self-Test 255
                Answers to the Self-Test 259

PART EIGHT: Late adulthood

Chapter 20   Physical development 261

                Chapter Summary 261
                Learning Objectives 263
                Key Terms 264
                Study Questions 265
                Self-Test 268
                Answers to the Self-Test 273

Chapter 21   Cognitive development 275

                Chapter Summary 275
                Learning Objectives 276
                Key Terms 277
                Study Questions 278
                Self-Test 280
                Answers to the Self-Test 284

Chapter 22   Social development 285

                Chapter Summary 285
                Learning Objectives 287
                Key Terms 288
                Study Questions 288
                Self-Test 290
                Answers to the Self-Test 294

Chapter 23   Death and dying 295

                Chapter Summary 295
                Learning Objectives 296
                Key Terms 297
                Study Questions 298
                Self-Test 301
                Answers to the Self-Test 305

HOW TO USE THIS GUIDE

This study guide consists of several components to assist you in mastering the contents of the text. Each of the 23 chapters of the <u>Study Guide</u> contains a detailed chapter summary of the material, learning objectives, key terms, study questions and a self-test on the material.

Chapter summaries are succinct, in depth presentations of the material. In the text, each chapter is divided into several sections. In our summary, each of these sections is summarized in a paragraph, and each key section heading and subheading is underlined.

Learning objectives detail what you should know once you have read and studied each chapter.

Key terms are terms boldfaced in the text and compiled at the end of each chapter. Pages where these terms appear are provided.

Study questions are essay and short answer questions on the material. Page numbers where correct responses may be located are included.

The self-test consists of completion, multiple-choice, and matching questions. Answers with corresponding page numbers are provided at the end of each chapter of the <u>Study Guide</u>. Together the study questions and self-test cover all the key concepts in a chapter.

TEXT ORGANIZATION

This text is organized into eight parts corresponding to stages of the lifecycle. Part 1, Introduction, includes an historical overview of a lifespan approach and a chapter on methods of study. Part 2, Foundations, discusses the roles of heredity and environment in development, and charts development from conception through birth. Each of the remaining six parts, Infancy, Early Childhood, Middle Childhood, Adolescence, Early and Middle Adulthood and Late Adulthood, contains chapters on physical development, cognitive development, and social and emotional development in each of these age periods.

STUDY TIPS

To be most effective in your study of this material, we suggest you do the following:

1. Read the chapter summary and learning objectives in the Study Guide first. This will orient you to the material, and alert you to concepts you should be looking for.

2. Before reading the chapter in detail, scan it for major sections and titles. While scanning the text, ask yourself what you will be learning. This process puts you into an active, rather than a passive, learning mode, and increases the chances that you will retain the material you read.

3. Look over the first section in the chapter. Examine the section heading. What are you to learn from this section? The learning objectives in the Study Guide will help you to identify what you should "take away" from the section.

4. Actively read the first section, looking for the answers to your questions.

5. Make notes in your guide on the responses to your questions, including the definitions of key terms.

6. Repeat steps 3, 4 and 5 for each section of the chapter.

7. After you have finished the chapter, quiz yourself using the study questions and self-test in the Study Guide, if you miss a question, reread the section it came from to understand why you might have missed it. Get together with classmates to quiz each other on the material. Having to explain concepts out loud is a good way of identifying what you do and do not understand.

8. Review the material in the chapter a few minutes each week. This will help you to retain the material longer for the exam.

Stephen J. Lepore

Wendy Kliewer

University of California, Irvine

CHAPTER SUMMARY

Chapter 1 defines and gives an historical overview of lifespan developmental psychology. Unlike earlier views of development, the lifespan perspective considers growth and change not only for children, but for people of all ages. This chapter covers predominant theories for various time periods ranging from the middle 20th century to the present.

The lifespan perspective on human development highlights important philosophical and scientific views that have contributed to the lifespan perspective. Precursors of the lifespan perspective can be traced to works by the early German philosophers Tetens and Carus, and the Belgian statistician Quetelet. Although presented over a century prior, American psychologists did not embrace this perspective until the 1970s. The lifespan perspective today points out the importance of the time period in which people develop, and suggests that life is divided into distinct stages.

Two contrasting views of human development are portrayed in Philosophical roots. Locke viewed nurture (e.g., how children are raised) as the most important determinant of development, while Rousseau believed that nature (e.g., inborn characteristics of children) was most central. Charles Darwin was one of the first people to support a theory of development with observational evidence. He is considered the scientific forefather of developmental psychology.

The early 20th century: developmental psychology as a fledgling science discusses the contributions of six important developmental psychologists. G. Stanley Hall is noted for establishing the psychological study of children. Binet and Simon devised the first standardized test of intelligence, and compiled norms of intelligence for different age groups. Gesell is known for documenting milestones of development, and he suggested that development is a result of natural forces, or maturation. Watson advanced the view among American psychologists that behaviors are learned, or conditioned, responses to the environment. He was a major proponent of studying observable behaviors. Sigmund Freud put forth an important theory of the psychosexual stages of development of humans. These include oral, anal, phallic and genital stages. The id, ego, superego, Oedipal and Electra conflicts are other important Freudian concepts.

Theoretical advancements are presented in The middle 20th century: theories of development. Learning theories discussed include social learning, operant learning and observational learning. Social learning theorists distinguish two kinds of drives: primary (biological) and secondary (learned), that are important for human development. Operant learning theorists, such as B.F. Skinner, believe that learning follows from reinforcement or punishment of behaviors. Observational learning, as proposed by Bandura, Walters and Mischel, happens through children's imitation of other people's actions. The ethological approach is distinct from learning theories, emphasizing the biological mechanisms underlying development. Bowlby's work on attachment stems from an ethological approach. Erik Erikson outlined eight stages of psychosocial development through which all humans are thought to progress. He proposed that various stages of the lifespan from one year to old age present unique psychological crises that individuals must resolve. Jean Piaget's theory depicts cognitive development as a result of interactions between maturational and environmental influences. He also described four stages of cognitive development that children proceed through from birth to maturity: sensorimotor, preoperational, concrete operational, and formal operational.

Theories in perspective indicates the importance of theories for guiding research and organizing results. Not all aspects of theories are correct and, frequently, old theories are retained in part or used to build new theories. The section on New theoretical approaches briefly describes new directions of developmental psychology. Information processing is an approach to understanding cognitive development based on a comparison of brain processes with computer processes. Advocates of the dialectal approach see development as a process of continual change emerging from crises. The influence of human settings and contexts are of concern to developmentalists with an ecological perspective. Sociobiologists emphasize the genetic basis of behaviors. New versions of old theories are created regularly by scholars. The original theories are changed as researchers attempt to integrate new information.

The chapter ends with a discussion of what developmental psychologists study. The definition of development, the nature of developmental change, the domains -- physical, cognitive, social-emotional -- of development, and the causes of development are addressed. Finally, a forecast of future topics, approaches and concerns of developmental psychology are discussed.

LEARNING OBJECTIVES

When you have finished studying Chapter 1 in both the text and this guide, you should be able to do the following:

1. Describe how the lifespan perspective of developmental psychology differs from approaches that only focus on child development.

2. Discuss the precursors of the lifespan perspective and the nature of the lifespan perspective today.

3. Compare Locke's "nurture" view of development with Rousseau's "nature" view of development, and discuss how ideas about heredity and environment have influenced theories of human development.

4. Describe the major contributions of Charles Darwin to the "science" of developmental psychology.

5. Discuss the contributions to the study of children made by G. Stanley Hall, Binet and Simon, Arnold Gesell, John Watson, and Sigmund Freud.

6. Define and describe the important aspects of social, operant, and observational learning theories.

7. Define ethology, and discuss its influence on the thinking of developmental psychologists.

8. Describe Erik Erikson's theory of psychosocial development, and note how this theory compares with Freud's theory of psychosexual development.

9. Describe Jean Piaget's theory of cognitive development.

10. Discuss the central ideas of the new theoretical perspectives -- information processing, dialectical, ecological -- on development.

11. Discuss how theories of development change over time.

12. Define development, and discuss how development differs from other forms of change.

13. Discuss the major features of the three domains of development -- physical, cognitive, and social.

14. Describe the factors developmental psychologists consider in the study of causes of development.

15. Discuss the probable concerns of future developmental psychologists.

KEY TERMS

Lifespan (p. 4)

INTRODUCTION

Nurture (p. 6)

Nature (p. 6)

Ontogeny (p. 6)

Phylogeny (p. 6)

Norms (p. 8)

Maturational (p. 8)

Classical conditioning (p. 8)

Behaviorism (p. 11)

Oral stage (p. 12)

Anal stage (p. 12)

Phallic stage (p. 12)

Oedipal conflict (p. 12)

Electra conflict (p. 12)

Latency period (p. 12)

Genital stage (p. 12)

Id (p. 12)

Ego (p. 12)

Superego (p. 12)

Primary (biological) drive (p. 13)

Secondary (learned) drive (p. 13)

Operant learning theory (p. 14)

Operant conditioning (p. 14)

Reinforcement (p. 14)

Punishment (p. 14)

INTRODUCTION

Behavior modification (p. 14)

Ethology (p. 14)

Critical period (p. 16)

Imprinting (p. 16)

Psychosexual development (p. 16)

Psychosocial development (p. 16)

Information processing (p. 20)

Dialectical (p. 21)

Ecological (p. 21)

Microsystem (p. 21)

Mesosystem (p. 21)

Macrosystem (p. 21)

Sociobiology (p. 22)

Neobehavioristic (p. 22)

Neo-Piagetian (p. 22)

Neo-Freudian (p. 23)

STUDY QUESTIONS

1. How does lifespan developmental psychology differ from child developmental psychology? (pp. 4-5)

2. Give a brief historical overview of the emergence of the lifespan perspective. (pp. 4-5)

3. According to the lifespan perspective, what factors affect individual development. (p. 5)

4. Who were Locke and Rousseau, and how did they influence the field of developmental psychology? (p. 6)

INTRODUCTION

5. Describe Charles Darwin's theory of evolution and its influence on the study of human development. (pp. 6-7)

6. Why was G. Stanley Hall's influence on the field of developmental psychology fairly limited? (p. 7)

7. How did Simon and Binet influence the study of intelligence? (p. 8)

8. Describe Gesell's conception of human development. (p. 8)

9. Describe the origins of behaviorism. (pp. 8-11)

10. What contribution did Watson make to the method of studying children? (pp. 10-11)

11. Identify and discuss the major components of Sigmund Freud's theory of development. (pp. 11-12)

12. Compare and contrast the three major learning theories of development -- social, operant, observational. (pp. 13-14)

13. How have developmental theorists been influenced by the study of ethology? (pp. 15-16)

14. Briefly describe Erik Erikson's theory of psychosocial development. (pp. 16-18)

INTRODUCTION

15. List and describe Erikson's eight developmental crises. (p. 17)

16. Discuss the major components of Jean Piaget's theory of cognitive development. (pp. 18-19)

17. List and describe Piaget's stages of cognitive development. (p. 19)

18. Indicate the important elements of the following modern theoretical approaches to the study of development: information processing, dialectical, ecological, sociobiological. (pp. 20-22)

19. How does developmental change differ from other forms of change? (p. 23)

SELF-TEST, CHAPTER 1

COMPLETION QUESTIONS

1. Developmental psychologists taking a _lifespan_ perspective believe that human development involves simultaneous growth and decline throughout life.

2. _Tetens_ and Carus were German philosophers who proposed that development is a lifelong process.

3. Quetelet presented data on the entire lifespan and emphasized the importance of general laws of development as well as _social_ and _historical_ change.

4. Research on children who grew up during the Great Depression demonstrated the importance of the _historical_ context within which people develop.

5. Locke saw _nurture_ as the driving force in development, while Rousseau emphasized _nature_.

6. Gesell observed children's growth and charted it on developmental timetables to support his view that development is _maturational_.

7. A dog can be taught to salivate to a bell, or a child to cry when he/she sees his/her favorite toy, using _classical_ conditioning.

8. Freud believed that infants in the _oral_ stage focus on the pleasures of sucking and taking food with mouth and tongue.

9. Stimuli that are regularly associated with primary (biological) drives that are basic to human survival, including hunger and thirst, themselves become the objects of secondary, or _learned_ drives.

10. A child who repeats an observed behavior is demonstrating _observational_ learning.

11. _ethology_ is the study of how animals behave in their natural environments.

12. Erik Erikson expanded Freud's theory of psychosexual development and developed his own theory of _psychosocial_ development.

13. How people take in information and remember it is the central question in the _information processing_ approach.

INTRODUCTION

14. Psychologists who take a _dialectic_ approach believe that development is a process of continual change emerging from crises and resolution.

MULTIPLE CHOICE

1. The view that development is mainly dependent upon natural or internal forces is favored by:

   a. Locke
   b. Watson
   c. Gesell
   d. Freud
   e. Binet

2. The view that development is mainly dependent upon nurture or environmental forces is favored by:

   a. Carus
   b. Watson
   c. Tetens
   d. Quetelet
   e. all of the above

3. Charles Darwin's theory of evolution changed the way scientists thought about:

   a. development of species
   b. development of societies
   c. development of human beings
   d. c only
   e. a, b, and c

4. On several successive days, a child is playing in the driveway near her parents' new car when the wind makes the car alarm sound off. Subsequently, she begins to act anxious when she must go for a drive in the car. What phenomenon does this illustrate?

   a. classical conditioning
   b. behavior modification
   c. operant conditioning
   d. car sickness
   e. learned drive

5. Circle the 3 theories that reflect Locke's and Watson's pro-nurture view of development.

   a. the oral stage in Freud's theory
   b. social learning theory
   c. ethology
   d. operant learning theory
   e. observational learning

6. The concept of "critical period" from the study of animals was borrowed to study which of the following processes in human development?

   a. the sensual satisfaction of infants who are breast-fed in early infancy
   b. a young boy's desire to kill his father and marry his mother
   c. a young girl's desire to replace her mother in her father's attention
   d. a child's attachment to his/her mother
   e. why children walk like ducks after they are born

7. During the sensorimotor stage, the child also is in which of the following stages?

   a. anal; autonomy versus shame
   b. oral; trust versus mistrust
   c. phallic; initiative versus guilt
   d. latency; industry versus inferiority
   e. genital; identity versus role confusion

8. Which of the following factors affecting development are of special concern to the ecological psychologist.

   a. how people accommodate to the environments in which they grow and live
   b. the network of ties between people and their immediate settings such as school or family c. legal, political, social, educational, and economic systems
   d. social class
   e. all of the above

9. Which of the following is NOT a characteristic of human development, according to developmental psychologists?

   a. change is systematic, not random
   b. development is permanent, not temporary
   c. development is both progressive and regressive
   d. development is related to a person's increasing age
   e. development ordinarily means improvement and increasing complexity, competence, and efficiency

INTRODUCTION

MATCHING

A. Match each statement with the appropriate theorist(s).

_c_ 1. psychological forefather of the study of children
_f_ 2. scientific forefather of developmental psychology
_g_ 3. believed that development is maturational
_d_ 4. asserted that sexuality starts at the beginning of life
_h_ 5. proposed that psychologists study observable behavior
_l_ 6. applied principles of operant learning theory to the study of children
_e_ 7. devised the first standardized test of intelligence
_m_ 8. demonstrated that animals are born with predispositions to learn behaviors during critical periods
_i_ 9. described the microsystems, mesosystems, and macrosystems that people live and grow in
_a_ 10. suggested that people watch how others behave and then sometimes imitate them as a way of learning

a. Bandura, Walters, and Mischel
b. Jean Piaget
c. G. Stanley Hall
d. Sigmund Freud
e. Binet and Simon
f. Charles Darwin
g. Gesell
h. Watson
i. Urie Bronfenbrenner
j. Carus
k. Locke
l. B.F. Skinner
m. Niko Tinbergen and Konrad Lorenz

B. Match the correct age with its corresponding period.

_h_ 1. early childhood
_b_ 2. infancy
_f_ 3. late adulthood
_c_ 4. early adulthood
_g_ 5. adolescence
_i_ 6. middle childhood
_e_ 7. middle adulthood

a. birth to age 7
b. birth to age 18 to 24 months
c. early twenties through the thirties
d. from 15 to 30 years
e. extends through the mid-fifties or mid-sixties
f. extends from the end of middle adulthood until death
g. early twenties
h. extends from infancy's end until age 5 or 6
i. extends from roughly age 6 to 11

ANSWERS TO THE SELF-TEST, CHAPTER 1

COMPLETION QUESTIONS

1. lifespan (p. 4)
2. Tetens (p. 4)
3. social, historical (p. 4)
4. historical (p. 5)
5. nurture, nature (p. 6)
6. maturational (p. 8)
7. classical (pp. 8-9)
8. oral (p. 12)
9. learned (p. 13)
10. observational (p. 14)
11. ethology (p. 14)
12. psychosocial (p. 16)
13. information processing (p. 20)
14. dialectical (p. 21)

MULTIPLE CHOICE

1. c (pp. 6-12)
2. e (pp. 4-11)
3. e (p. 6)
4. a (p. 8)
5. b, d, e (p. 14)
6. d (p. 16)
7. b (pp. 17-19)
8. e (pp. 21-22)
9. c (p. 23)

MATCHING

A.

1. c (p. 7)
2. f (p. 6)
3. g (p. 8)
4. d (pp. 11-12)
5. h (pp. 8-11)
6. l (p. 14)
7. e (p. 7)
8. m (p. 16)
9. i (p. 21)
10. a (p. 14)

B.

1. h (p. 26)
2. b (p. 26)
3. f (p. 26)
4. c (p. 26)
5. g (p. 26)
6. i (p. 26)
7. e (p. 26)

CHAPTER SUMMARY

Chapter 2 describes the scientific method and how it is used to
study human development across the lifespan. Topics covered
include the choices developmental psychologists must make to
design research, collect and analyze data, and interpret their
results. The chapter also discusses problems in doing a study and
research ethics.

The scientific method is the general approach that developmental
psychologists use to test a hypothesis about some aspect of
development. A hypothesis is an "educated guess" or prediction
that grows out of findings of another study, or is based on
formal theory. A hypothesis is tested against reality by
systematically collecting data, or facts, about the phenomenon of
interest. Once data are collected, they are analyzed
statistically to determine whether they support or disconfirm the
hypothesis. Finally, the study may be replicated, with different
subjects, different procedures, or by different researchers to
test the strength of the original findings.

The section on Research designs discusses basic methods of
studying people of different ages. In a longitudinal research
design, a sample is followed over an extended period, as they get
older. In a cross-sectional research design, separate samples of
different ages are studied. Cross-sectional research is
problematic if the samples being compared are not similar on all
variables except age. If samples differ in ways other than by
age (e.g., by sex or physical health), then any observed
differences between groups' behavior may be caused by those other
factors and not by development. However, if samples are
carefully selected cross-sectional research can provide a sense
of developmental change more quickly and cheaply than
longitudinal research. Longitudinal research has several
disadvantages resulting from loss of subjects, practice effects,
and lack of generalizability. However, if done properly,
longitudinal research can reveal important continuities,
discontinuities, and patterns of change with age. Cohort
sequential research design combines the best elements of
longitudinal and cross-sectional strategies. This method can be
used to differentiate three kinds of influences on development:
1) age-related; 2) history-related; and 3) non-normative.

Researchers also must consider whether to design a correlational
versus experimental study. Each method has its benefits and
limitations. In a correlational design, researchers measure
relations among naturally occurring events, or things. Because
it is difficult to disentangle cause from effect with this
method, researchers often will attempt an experimental design. In
an experimental design, researchers manipulate environments and
look at the effects of their manipulation on behavior. This
method also has limitations, and is frequently neither practical

nor ethical for use with human subjects.

The section on <u>Collecting data</u> describes various data collection methods: naturalistic or structured observation, interviews and questionnaires, or tests. The section also discusses the advantages, disadvantages and techniques of each of these methods. Researchers conduct <u>naturalistic observations</u> by focusing on naturally occurring spontaneous behaviors of subjects doing everyday routines. Researchers conduct <u>structured observations</u> by focusing on behavior in situations that have been set up by the researcher. <u>Interviews and questionnaires</u> provide data in the form of words rather than observed actions, while standardized <u>tests</u> offer researchers easily and objectively collected data that can be compared to preestablished responses. As with research design, the choice of observational method is determined in part by the hypothesis being tested and the resources of the researcher.

The section on <u>Recording and coding the data</u> lists a variety of options for recording data during the data collection process, and for transforming the recorded data into categories or numbers to be used in analysis.

<u>Problems in doing a study</u> is subdivided into three major areas of concern: <u>sampling</u>, <u>researcher bias</u>, and <u>reliability and replicability</u>. In order to use data to make general statements about development, researchers must <u>sample</u> enough people and people who are representative of the entire population. <u>Researcher bias</u> can affect data collection and influence results. This can be controlled if the researcher collecting the data is "blind" to the hypothesis or the study, or to the subject's condition. Finally, the data must be <u>reliable</u>, or objective, reflections of reality. And, the results should be <u>replicated</u> if the same study is conducted at a different time and with different subjects. Replicability is typically a problem if data were not reliably collected or coded.

<u>Analyzing data</u> usually requires statistics to provide the following: a) descriptions of subjects or their behaviors; b) tests of differences between average scores of different groups; and c) information about relations between variables. <u>Descriptive analysis</u> can describe people's behavior by indicating the frequency of the behavior, or the average frequency of the behavior. A graphic plot of the frequencies can reveal whether the sample was large enough and representative enough to allow for further statistical analyses. One further analysis might be to test whether the difference between the average scores on two groups' behavior is <u>statistically significant</u>. <u>Statistical relations</u> can also be explored. To analyze the degree to which two variables are related, a researcher can analyze the correlation between them.

Once the data have been collected and analyzed, there remains a final task of <u>interpreting results</u>. This involves explaining what the results mean and clarifying confusing and inconsistent outcomes. Particular care must be taken if the researcher wishes to infer a causal relation between variables.

The chapter concludes with a discussion of <u>Research ethics</u>. Important ethical considerations in conducting research are: a) the protection of subjects' rights; b) the provision of safe procedures; and c) the benefit to science and society.

LEARNING OBJECTIVES

When you have finished studying Chapter 2 in both the text and this guide, you should be able to do the following:

1. Explain the key features of the scientific method.

2. Describe longitudinal, cross-sectional, and cohort-sequential research designs. List the pros and cons of each design.

3. Describe correlational and experimental designs. List the pros and cons of each design.

4. Discuss the difference between naturalistic and structured observations.

5. Indicate how observational studies differ from studies that use interviews, tests, and questionnaires.

6. Discuss the problems of sampling, researcher bias, reliability and replicability.

7. Discuss the ways that statistics are used to analyze data.

8. Discuss the care researchers must take in interpreting their results.

9. Discuss the ethical concerns of researchers studying human development.

KEY TERMS

Scientific method (p. 30)

Hypothesis (p. 30)

INTRODUCTION

Data (p. 30)

Longitudinal research design (p. 30)

Cross-sectional research design (p. 30)

Practice effects (p. 31)

Cohort (p. 31)

Cohort-sequential research design (p. 31)

Correlational design (p. 34)

Experimental design (p. 35)

Control group (p. 35)

Interventions (p. 35)

Naturalistic observation (p. 36)

Structured observation (p. 36)

Validity (p. 41)

Case study (p. 43)

Representative sample (p. 43)

Robust (p. 44)

Double-blind study (p. 44)

Reliability (p. 44)

Replicability (p. 44)

Interval scale (p. 45)

Mean (p. 45)

Normal distribution (p. 45)

Growth curve (p. 46)

Statistical significance (p. 46)

Correlation (p. 46)

INTRODUCTION

STUDY QUESTIONS

1. List and explain the central features of the scientific method. (p. 30)

2. Give several examples of hypotheses. (p. 30)

3. Describe longitudinal, cross-sectional, and cohort-sequential research designs. (pp. 30-34)

4. Why is it important to have comparable samples in a cross-sectional study? (pp. 30-31)

5. What are the major weaknesses of a longitudinal research design? Focus on drop out, practice effects and cohort problems. (pp. 30-31)

6. Discuss the three kinds of influences on development that can be distinguished using a cohort sequential research design (pp. 31-34)

7. Describe correlational and experimental designs. (pp. 34-36)

8. What are the problems in inferring causality from correlational data? (pp. 34-36)

9. List the major advantages and disadvantages associated with using an experimental design. (pp. 34-36)

10. Discuss the difference between naturalistic and structured observations. (pp. 36-39)

INTRODUCTION

11. Indicate how observational studies differ from studies that use interviews, tests, and questionnaires. (pp. 39-42)

12. What problems do researchers face in interviewing people. How is interviewing different with young children versus adults? (pp. 39-40)

13. What are the main issues of sampling in research? (pp. 43-44)

14. How does a case sample differ from a representative sample? (pp. 43-44)

15. What is researcher bias, and how can it be controlled?
     (p. 44)

16. What is reliability, and how does it relate to
     replicability? (pp. 44-45)

17. How can descriptive analyses indicate whether a sample was
     representative of the normal population? (pp. 45-46)

18. What does the term "statistically significant differences"
     refer to? (p. 46)

INTRODUCTION

19. Define correlation, and give a rough sketch of a positive
    correlation between weight and height for five people.
    (pp. 46-47)

20. What must researchers consider when interpreting their
    results? (pp. 47-48)

21. Discuss the ethical concerns of researchers studying human
    development. (pp. 48-49)

SELF-TEST, CHAPTER 2

COMPLETION QUESTIONS

1. In a _longitud_ research design, a sample is followed over an extended period.

2. In a _cross-sectional_ research design, separate samples of different ages are studied.

3. After years of taking tests, the subjects in a longitudinal sample will show _practice_ effects.

4. _Cohort_ is the term used to describe a sample of people who were all born in the same year.

5. Observations of behavior and relationships as they occur in real life is an advantage of a _correlation_ research design.

6. In _naturalistic_ observations, researchers try hard not to influence the behavior of the subjects they are studying.

7. _Structured_ observations have the advantages of giving researchers some control over the situation and of giving them a chance to look at how different people behave in a single, standard situation.

8. Questionnaires or _test/interviews_ allow researcher to compare data from different subjects, and to compare an individual's performance to norms.

9. An _interview_ is a quick way to get information, and the only way to assess conscious intentions and attitudes.

10. A _representative_ sample is comprised of subjects who represent the entire population researchers are interested in studying.

11. Observations are thought to be _reliable_ if several different observers agree on the observation.

12. When data are quantitative and form an _interval_ scale, researchers can calculate the mean frequency for the sample.

13. Researchers must not claim that one variable caused another when they have documented only the two are _correlated_.

INTRODUCTION

MULTIPLE CHOICE

1. The scientific method includes which of the following steps?

   a. development of a hypothesis from a relevant theory
   b. development of a hypothesis from a hunch guess, or prediction about the world
   c. collecting data
   d. analyzing data with statistics
   e. all of the above

2. Which of the following research designs shows average developmental changes with age, but does not indicate individual growth curves or temporal relations?

   a. cross-sectional
   b. cohort sequential
   c. longitudinal
   d. experimental
   e. correlational

3. Which of the following is NOT generally a problem of longitudinal research designs?

   a. practice effects
   b. non-comparable samples
   c. generalizing findings to different cohorts
   d. amount of time required to do study
   e. none of the above

4. Circle the 3 influences on development that can be differentiated with a cohort sequential research design?

   a. biological factors closely linked with chronological age
   b. psychological factors
   c. unique events
   d. environmental factors closely linked with historical eras
   e. social status of parents

5. Which of the following statements about an experimental design is FALSE?

   a. researchers manipulate variables of interest b. experimental designs require at least two groups of subjects -- a control group and an experimental group
   c. behaviors of different groups are observed and measured without any intervention by the researcher
   d. subjects are assigned to either the control group or experimental group at random
   e. experiments can take place in either a laboratory or in natural environments

6. Which of the following statements about naturalistic and structured observations is TRUE?

    a. both methods raise concerns about the intrusiveness of observers and their equipment
    b. structured observations are always done in a laboratory
    c. developmental psychologists taking an ethological approach are likely to conduct structured observations
    d. naturalistic observations are better than structured ones because developmental psychologist study natural behavior
    e. both a and d

7. Which of the following characteristics describe a skillful interviewer?

    a. asks leading questions to get a good answer
    b. realizes the first response is the best
    c. changes the style and tone of the interview to match the subject's personality
    d. never trusts the accuracy of young children's responses
    e. none of the above

8. Test validity refers to:

    a. how representative a sample is
    b. how well prepared, sensitive, and flexible an interviewer is when administering a questionnaire
    c. how accurately a test measures what it is supposed to measure
    d. how well two measures correlate
    e. all of the above

9. The case-study method has limited usefulness because:

    a. the researcher collects too much data on each subject
    b. data drawn from this method may not generalize to other groups of people
    c. subject's privacy is invaded
    d. data are often superficial
    e. data are not collected systematically

10. Researcher bias refers to:

    a. prejudice against researchers from minority groups
    b. the greater number of male than female faculty in psychology departments
    c. the problem of subjectivity in naturalistic observation
    d. the tendency of experimenters to let their hypotheses affect their data collecting
    e. problems in data collection that result from using researchers who do not know subjects' conditions

INTRODUCTION

11. Which of the following statements about the ethics of doing research on humans is TRUE?

    a. research that only uses questionnaires is ethical
    b. subjects should give their consent to participate, but should not be informed about the nature of the study until after they participate
    c. it is ethical for researchers to lie to subjects about the research if the truth is too damaging psychologically
    d. some investigations done in the 1930s, 40s, and 50s probably would not be approved by human subjects committees in the 1980s
    e. data collected by unethical means are never published

MATCHING

Match the following statements with the research design or data collection method they characterize.

 1. subjects observed without researcher intervening; cannot be used to determine cause and effect
 2. questions posed to children and adults; interviewees are biased
 3. same assessment given to all subjects; data are limited to preestablished responses
 4. different samples observed at different ages; does not indicate individual growth curves
____ 5. data not restricted to preestablished test responses; does not get at underlying attitudes

a. correlational research design
b. experimental research design
c. cross-sectional research design
d. longitudinal research design
e. structured observation
f. naturalistic observation
g. questionnaire of test
h. interview

ANSWERS TO THE SELF-TEST, CHAPTER 2

COMPLETION QUESTIONS

1. longitudinal (p. 30)
2. cross-sectional (p. 30)
3. practice (p. 31)
4. cohort (p. 31)
5. correlational (p. 36)
6. naturalistic (p. 36)
7. structured (p. 38)
8. tests (p. 42)
9. interview (p. 42)
10. representative (p. 43)
11. reliable (p. 44)
12. interval (p. 45)
13. correlated (p. 48)

MULTIPLE CHOICE

1. e (p. 30)
2. a (p. 36)
3. b (pp. 30-31)
4. a, c, d (pp. 31-34)
5. c (pp. 35-36)
6. a (pp. 36-39)
7. e (pp. 39-40)
8. c (p. 41)
9. b (p. 43)
10. d (p. 44)
11. a (pp. 48-49)

MATCHING

1. a (p. 36)
2. h (p. 42)
3. g (p. 42)
4. c (p. 36)
5. e (p. 42)

CHAPTER SUMMARY

Chapter 3, Heredity and environment, outlines the biological and environmental factors affecting development.

The section Nature-nurture interaction indicates that both heredity and environment contribute to human development. Genetic material, termed genotype, is biologically determined; the expression of that genetic material in physical and behavior traits, termed phenotype, is strongly influenced by the environment. Models of gene-environment interaction presents several ways in which heredity and environment affect each other. The reaction range model demonstrates how characteristics of the environment (e.g., enrichment) influence how genotypes are expressed. Potential may be expressed or repressed depending on environmental influences, and some characteristics are more susceptible to influence than others. A second model concerns the "canalization" of traits. Traits tightly controlled by genes are "canalized". Traits not canalized are more susceptible to environmental influences. A third model states that a person's genotype affects the environment by (1) evoking particular responses from the environment, and (2) actively seeking stimulating and compatible environments. With age, the role of environment becomes more important and genotype less important in predicting IQ.

Genetic building blocks include DNA, RNA, and chromosomes. DNA contains the chemical instructions for making a human being. Information on DNA molecules is transferred to RNA, then transported into the cytoplasm of the cell where construction from proteins begins. Meiosis, special cell division in which crossover of genetic material occurs, is necessary for conception. Zygotes are comprised of 46 chromosomes -- 23 each from a male and female. Most genetic material is carried on 22 pairs of chromosomes. The remaining two determine the child's sex: XX forms a female and XY forms a male.

Physical characteristics are inherited. Genetic inheritance is determined by dominant and recessive genes, and recessive traits need two recessive genes to be expressed. Most physical characteristics involve more than one gene. Extreme environmental conditions can affect the expression of physical characteristics.

Behavioral traits are also inherited, are more susceptible to environmental influence than are physical characteristics, and involve more than one gene. There are several methods of studying inheritance of traits. Twin studies are one method. Monozygotic twins have identical genetic material, while dizygotic twins share no more genetic material than any two siblings. Similarities and differences between monozygotic twins and dizygotic twins help to identify traits under environmental versus genetic control. Analyzing family trees and comparing adopted children with their biological and adoptive parents are two additional ways of determining which traits are inherited versus acquired. Experimental interventions have been attempted to change people's intelligence. Aspects of personality and temperament appear to be partly inherited, including activity level, sociability, empathy, nurturance, altruism, adaptability, dominance, assertiveness, self-confidence and depression. Intelligence is genetically influenced, but can vary up to 25 IQ points depending on the environment.

Several types of physical and behavioral disorders are inherited. These physical disorders include Down's syndrome, sickle-cell anemia, phenylketonuria (PKU) and sex-linked defects such as hemophilia, color blindness, and baldness. Some behavioral disorders such as schizophrenia and dyslexia are inherited; minor behavior problems also have genetic components. Maternal blood tests, amniocentesis, and ultrasound are used to test for defects in a developing child.

LEARNING OBJECTIVES

When you have finished studying Chapter 3 in both the text and this guide, you should be able to do the following:

1. Describe the models of gene-environment interaction and explain how they differ from each other.

2. Describe the process of genetic encoding during conception.

3. State how physical traits are inherited, and explain the role of the environment in the expression of physical characteristics.

4. Name four methods of studying the inheritance of behavioral traits.

5. Discuss the role of heredity in the expression of temperament and personality.

6. Explain how heredity and environment interact to influence intelligence.

7. Note physical defects that are inherited and which groups of children are most at risk for these disorders.

8. Discuss the role of genetic factors in behavioral disorders such as schizophrenia and dyslexia.

9. Cite common methods of testing for genetic defects.

KEY TERMS

Genotype (p. 54)

Phenotype (p. 54)

Expression (p. 54)

Reaction range (p. 55)

Canalized (p. 56)

Chromosomes (p. 59)

DNA (p. 59)

Mitosis (p. 59)

RNA (p. 59)

Meiosis (p. 59)

Testes (p. 59)

Ovaries (p. 59)

Sperm (p. 59)

FOUNDATIONS

Ova (p. 59)

Homologous (p. 59)

Crossover (p. 59)

Autosomes (p. 59)

Genes (p. 59)

Conception (p. 59)

Zygote (p. 59)

X Chromosome (p. 60)

Y Chromosome (p. 60)

Recessive (p. 60)

Dominant (p. 60)

Polygenic (p. 60)

Monozygotic (MZ) (p. 61)

Dizygotic (DZ) (p. 61)

Concordance (p. 62)

Personality (p. 64)

Temperament (p. 64)

Down's syndrome (p. 67)

Sickle-cell anemia (p. 69)

Phenylketonuria (PKU) (p. 69)

Sex-linked (p. 69)

Schizophrenia (p. 70)

Dyslexia (p. 70)

Amnioscentesis (p. 70)

Ultrasound (p. 70)

Chorionic villus biopsies (p. 71)

STUDY QUESTIONS

1. Using intelligence and sociability as examples, compare the role of heredity with environment in the reaction range and canalization models of gene-environment interaction. (pp. 55-57)

2. Describe the ways a person's genotype affects the environment. (pp. 57-58)

3. Discuss the advantages and disadvantages of using twins, family trees, and adopted children to study the inheritance of traits. (pp. 61-64)

4. Describe the role of genetics in the expression of personality and temperament. (pp. 64-65)

5. Cite evidence for the inheritance of intelligence. (pp. 65-66)

6.   Define sex-linked defects, and describe how these are transferred genetically. Give examples of common sex-linked defects. (pp. 69-70)

7.   Describe the role of genetics in the expression of physical and behavioral disorders. (pp. 67-70)

8.   Describe Down's syndrome and it's causes. What theories have been advanced to explain why older women are more likely to bear a Down's syndrome child? (pp. 67-69)

9.   What are some advantages and disadvantages of testing for birth defects? (pp. 70-71)

SELF-TEST, CHAPTER 3

COMPLETION QUESTIONS

1. _____ is the expression of a person's genetic inheritance in visible characteristics and behavior.

2. The _____ in each human cell contains the chemical instructions for building a complete human being.

3. The new cell formed by 23 chromosomes each from the male and female is called a _____.

4. Most of the genetic code for development is carried on 22 pairs of chromosomes called _____.

5. Physical and behavioral characteristics involving more than one gene are called _____.

6. _____ twins develop from one fertilized egg by mitosis; _____ twins develop from two eggs.

7. An infant's natural disposition or style of activity is called _____.

8. Individuals suffering from Down's syndrome have _____ chromosomes.

9. _____ is a metabolic disorder in which children cannot make an enzyme necessary for digestion.

10. Children of schizophrenic parents are _____ times more likely to become schizophrenic adults compared to children of non-schizophrenic parents.

MULTIPLE CHOICE

1. Which of the following traits is MOST vulnerable to environmental effects?

    a. schizophrenia
    b. IQ
    c. temperament
    d. height
    e. hair color

2. If both parents have brown eyes, the chance that their
    child will have blue eyes cannot exceed _____ percent.

    a. 25
    b. 33
    c. 50
    d. 67
    e. 75

3. Sarah and her brother James are twins. Which of the
    following statements about their development is TRUE?

    a. they developed from one fertilized egg; they have the
        same phenotype
    b. they developed from one fertilized egg; they have the
        same genotype
    c. they developed from two eggs; they have the same
        phenotype
    d. they developed from two eggs; they have the same
        genotype
    e. none of the above

4. Which of the following statements regarding genetic control
    of traits is FALSE?

    a. physical traits are under tighter genetic control than
        are behavioral traits
    b. in general, as a child ages, the influence of genetics on
        traits decreases
    c. most physical characteristics involve only one gene,
        while most behavioral characteristics involve more than
        one gene
    d. extreme environmental conditions (e.g., diet, health,
        living conditions) can affect how physical
        characteristics are expressed
    e. none of the above

5. A scientist was interested in studying the role of genetics
    in aggression. Which of the following methods would provide
    the clearest picture of the genetic (versus environmental)
    contributions to aggression?

    a. comparing dizygotic twins reared apart
    b. comparing monozygotic twins reared apart
    c. comparing adopted children with their biological and
        adoptive parents
    d. comparing dizygotic twins reared together
    e. comparing monozygotic twins reared together

FOUNDATIONS

6. Children's temperaments

    a. have no genetic basis
    b. are stable only through the first six months of life
    c. are easily predicted by knowing parents' temperaments
    (d) interact with the responses of others to affect
        personality development
    e. none of the above

7. Sickle-cell anemia

    a. is more common among US whites than among US blacks
    b. is always life threatening
    c. is adaptive in areas where malaria exists
    d. affects about 10% of the US population
    e. is similar to hemophilia

8. Which of the following statements concerning IQ is FALSE?

    a. identical twins reared apart have closer IQ scores than
       fraternal twins reared apart
    b. identical twins reared apart have closer IQ scores than
       fraternal twins reared together
    c. identical twins reared together have closer IQ scores
       than identical twins reared apart
    (d.) fraternal twins reared apart have much closer IQ scores
        than siblings reared apart
    e. none of the above

9. Which of the following statements concerning Down's Syndrome
    is FALSE?

    a. Down's syndrome can be identified by testing a mother's
       amniotic fluid
    b. Down's syndrome is caused by an excess chromosome
    (c.) as women age, the risk of conceiving a Down's Syndrome
        child decreases
    d. males are responsible for the genetic abnormality leading
       to Down's Syndrome up to a third of the time
    e. manifestations of Down's Syndrome include retarded mental
       and motor development

10. Sex-linked defects

    a. usually are carried on the Y chromosome
    b. are more common in women than in men
    c. include color blindness and schizophrenia
    (d.) usually are carried by recessive genes
    e. all of the above

MATCHING

Match each statement with the correct letter below.

_____ 1. suggested twins should be studied to understand the
           contributions of heredity and environment
_____ 2. model that explains how genotype and phenotype are
           related in different environments
_____ 3. normal cell division
_____ 4. persons sharing identical genetic material
_____ 5. a sex-linked defect
_____ 6. test for genetic defects performed as early as the
           10th week of pregnancy
_____ 7. problem with reading and spelling affecting people
           with normal intelligence
_____ 8. traits predicted by more than one gene
_____ 9. genetic similarity
_____ 10. parallel pairs of chromosomes

a. amniocentesis   m. homologous
b. autosomes   n. meiosis
c. baldness   o. mitosis
d. canalization   p. Monozygotic twins
e. chorionic villus biopsies   q. Piaget
f. concordance   r. PKU
g. crossover   s. polygenic
h. Darwin   t. reaction range
i. discordance   u. schizophrenia
j. Dizygotic twins   v. siblings
k. dyslexia   w. sickle-cell anemia
l. Galton

ANSWERS TO THE SELF-TEST, CHAPTER 3

COMPLETION QUESTIONS

1. Phenotype (p. 54)
2. DNA (p. 59)
3. zygote (p. 59)
4. autosomes (p. 59)
5. polygenic (p. 60)
6. Monozygotic; Dizygotic (p. 61)
7. temperament (p. 64)
8. 47 (p. 67)
9. Phenylketonuria (PKU) (p. 69)
10. 15 (p. 70)

MULTIPLE CHOICE

1. a (p. 56)
2. a (p. 60)
3. e (pp. 61-62)
4. c (pp. 55-58)
5. b (pp. 61-63)
6. d (pp. 64-65)
7. c (p. 69)
8. d (p. 66)
9. c (pp. 67-69)
10. d (pp. 69-70)

MATCHING

1. l (p. 61)
2. t (p. 55)
3. o (p. 59)
4. p (p. 61)
5. c (pp. 69-70)
6. e (p. 71)
7. k (p. 70)
8. s (p. 60)
9. f (p. 62)
10. m (p. 59)

CHAPTER SUMMARY

Chapter 4, Prenatal development and birth, traces fetal development from conception through the birthing process. Stages of prenatal development and how pregnancy affects parents are discussed. Environmental influences on the fetus are outlined, as well as stages of delivery and birth.

The section Beginning new life discusses parents' choices about having children, the process of conception, and barriers to fertility. As a result of better contraception and recent social pressures on women, parents' choices about family size have changed; more couples are choosing not to have any children, or to restrict family size to two offspring. Conception occurs when a mature female egg (ovum) is fertilized by a man's sperm in the three days after ovulation. Infertility has several causes, but nearly half of the cases can be helped. About 60% of infertility problems are attributed to women. Solutions include surgery, medication, artificial insemination, and methods of alternative reproduction such as in vitro fertilization, surrogate mothering, and ovum transfer.

The three stages of prenatal development and the effects of pregnancy on parents are discussed in the section Prenatal development. The two-week germinal stage begins when the ovum is fertilized and ends when the zygote attaches to the wall of the uterus. Organs form during the embryonic stage -- from the second to the eighth week of pregnancy. During the remainder of the pregnancy -- the fetal stage -- growth occurs and organs and muscles begin to function. In the third month eyelids form and are sealed shut, the roof of the mouth closes, kidneys are functioning, fluid is breathed in and out of the lungs, nerves connect to muscles and reflexive kicking occurs, and male sexual organs develop. Growth occurs more quickly than any other time during the fourth month. Finger and foot prints are formed, female sexual organs develop, and the placenta produces hormones that prepare the mother's body to produce milk. During the fifth month, sweat glands, eyelashes and brows, head hair, and downy body hair appear. Eyelids first open in the sixth month. Also, intestines descend into the abdomen, cartilage develops into bone, and the six cell layers in the cerebral cortex develop. In the seventh month, a fetus has a 50 percent chance of survival outside of the womb. Now the brain begins regulating breathing, body temperature, and swallowing, and many reflexes are established. Chances of survival outside of the womb increase to 85 percent in the eighth month, although the lungs and digestive and immune systems are immature. Nerve cells in the brain develop branches and neurotransmitters. Growth slows down in the final month. The fetus's position shifts and settles head down in the uterus. Full-term pregnancies last 38 weeks and are often accompanied by emotional and physical strains on parents.

Many factors in the prenatal environment affect the fetus. A mother's emotional state can affect fetal development, although the exact nature of the effects is unknown. Diabetes, Ph incompatibility, and rubella are three illnesses that endanger fetal health. A mother's nutrition is important to fetal development, particularly adequate protein. Women should gain at least 24 pounds when pregnant. Maternal age can influence fetal survival and birth complications. The best time physiologically to have a child is between 22 and 29. Older women may have difficulty conceiving and delivering, and have an increased probability of having a Down's syndrome child. Teenage mothers are more likely to have low birth weight children. Maternal employment may affect fetal weight if women are required to stand for long periods of time during their third trimester. Parity, the number of children a woman already has borne, affects prenatal development. Later born infants may have advantages over first borns.

External factors, teratogens, such as drugs, smoking, alcohol, and radiation, have profound effects on fetal development. Drugs can cross the placenta and can cause severe deformities. For example, mothers who ingest Thalidomide can produce infants without arms and legs. In spite of the risks, many pregnant women continue to use drugs. Smoking exposes the fetus to many toxic substances, affects fetal birth weight, and possibly has long-term effects on performance. Maternal alcohol consumption can cause fetal alcohol syndrome in which children are born with physical and mental deformities. Alcohol may be especially dangerous in the last trimester of pregnancy. Radiation may also affect fetal development by causing mutation in genetic material.

The "self-righting" tendency humans have is discussed under Prenatal vulnerability. Even when exposed to possible harm, most fetuses develop normally. When damage does occur, the severity is affected by (1) the constitution of the fetus, (2) the time of exposure, and (3) the amount of exposure. There is also a "self-cleansing" tendency. Severely malformed fetuses are spontaneously aborted in the first trimester.

Labor has three stages. Uterine contractions, which stretch the cervix to four inches, mark the first stage. This lasts an average of 14 hours for the first baby. Stage two, crowning, begins when the crown of the infant's head appears and does not recede. It ends when the baby is out of the birth canal, and lasts about two hours. Afterbirth is pushed out in the third stage.

The final section discusses changing attitudes toward childbirth. Lamaze training in breathing and relaxation in preparation for birth involves the pregnant woman and her coach, and is recommended by most obstetricians. Even with Lamaze training, most deliveries involve pain medication for the mother. These medications can affect the infant after birth. Leboyer has suggested a "gentle birth" method consisting of soft lights, quiet voices, a warm room, and gentle handling.

LEARNING OBJECTIVES

When you have finished studying Chapter 4 in both the text and this guide, you should be able to do the following:

1. Describe how parent's choices regarding child rearing have changed in the last two decades, and note factors responsible for these changes.

2. Describe the process of conception.

3. State the causes of infertility and solutions to these problems.

4. Chart the growth occurring in each month of prenatal development.

5. List the emotional and physical strains on mothers and fathers during pregnancy.

6. Discuss how a mother's emotional state, her health, age, type of work, parity and her nutritional status affect the prenatal development of the fetus.

7. Cite the influence of teratogens -- drugs, alcohol, smoking, and radiation -- on prenatal development.

8. Note the three factors affecting the severity of damage by harmful substances to the fetus.

9. Discuss what happens during each stage of labor.

10. Identify how attitudes toward childbirth have changed in the past two decades, and the effects on children of new birth procedures.

KEY TERMS

Ovulate (p. 77)

Oocyte (p. 77)

FOUNDATIONS

Fallopian tube (p. 77)

Uterus (p. 77)

Spermatozoa (p. 77)

Cervix (p. 78)

Infertility (p. 78)

Pelvic inflammatory disease (PID) (p. 78)

Artificial insemination (p. 80)

Alternative reproduction (p. 80)

In vitro fertilization (p. 80)

Test-tube baby (p. 80)

Laparoscopy (p. 80)

Surrogate mothering (p. 80)

Ovum transfer (p. 80)

Germinal stage (p. 81)

Embryonic stage (p. 81)

Fetal stage (p. 81)

Morula (p. 82)

Totipotent (p. 82)

Blastula (p. 82)

Blastocyst (p. 82)

Chorion (p. 82)

Amnion (p. 82)

Placenta (p. 82)

Villi (p. 82)

Implant (p. 82)

Embryo (p. 82)

FOUNDATIONS

Ectoderm (p. 82)

Primitive streak (p. 82)

Endoderm (p. 82)

Mesoderm (p. 82)

Umbilical cord (p. 82)

Cephalocaudal (p. 83)

Proximodistal (p. 84)

Ossification (p. 84)

Quickening (p. 85)

Lanugo (p. 85)

Vernix (p. 85)

Neonatology (p. 86)

Fetology (p. 86)

Hydrocephaly (p. 86)

Alveoli (p. 86)

Oxytocin (p. 87)

Toxemia (p. 89)

Diabetes (p. 90)

Rh incompatibility (p. 90)

Rubella (p. 91)

Parity (p. 92)

Teratology (p. 93)

Teratogen (p. 93)

Mutation (p. 93)

Phocomelia (p. 93)

Fetal alcohol syndrome (p. 95)

FOUNDATIONS

Microcephaly (p. 96)

Self-righting tendency (p. 96)

Labor (p. 98)

Crowning (p. 98)

Afterbirth (p. 99)

Epidural anesthesia (p. 100)

Gentle birth (p. 101)

STUDY QUESTIONS

1. Describe how parents' choices about having children have changed in recent years. What factors account for these changes? (pp. 76-77)

2. Discuss the causes of and treatments for infertility. (pp. 78-80)

3. Describe the major activity occurring during each of the 3 stages of prenatal development. (pp. 81-87)

4. Cite advantages and disadvantages of having a first child after age 35. (p. 92)

5. What are some common teratogens pregnant women should be concerned about? Describe the effects of these teratogens on prenatal development. (pp. 93-96)

6. Discuss the factors that determine the severity of effects of harmful substances on fetal development. (pp. 96-97)

7. How have attitudes toward childbirth changed in the last few decades? Have these changes affected children's health? (pp. 99-101)

SELF-TEST, CHAPTER 4

COMPLETION QUESTIONS

1. The _____ germinal stage of prenatal development begins when the ovum is fertilized and ends when the zygote attaches to the wall of the uterus.

2. Development starts at the head and moves to the tail, in _____ order.

3. _____ is a new medical specialty devoted to treating problems in fetuses before birth.

4. The tendency for a fetus to develop normally under all but the most damaging conditions is termed a _____-_____ tendency.

5. The drug _____ was responsible for the development of seal limbs in infants, a condition known as _____.

6. Sperm live for _____ hours or so after ejaculation; the ovum is receptive for _____ to _____ hours.

7. One cause of infertility is the sexually transmitted _____ _____ disease, which leaves scars on the woman's fallopian tubes, ovaries, and uterus.

8. Men account for _____ percent of all fertility problems.

9. The placenta is connected to the embryo by the _____ _____.

10. _____ is the study of structural and functional deformities in children.

MULTIPLE CHOICE

1. During ovulation

    a. an oocyte is released into a fallopian tube
    b. an oocyte is released from the ovary
    c. an ovum is released from the uterus
    d. an ovum is released into the ovary
    e. an ovum is released into a fallopian tube

2. Treatments for infertility include all but which of the following?

    a. tying off varicose veins in a man's testicles
    b. unblocking the uterus
    c. artificial insemination
    d. in vitro fertilization
    e. ovum transfer

3. The embryonic stage

    a. is the first stage of prenatal development
    b. lasts about 2 months
    c. is when lanugo begins to grow over the body
    d. is when the heart and lungs form
    e. all of the above

4. Common responses of an expectant mother to her pregnancy include all but which of the following?

    a. concern over the well-being of the developing fetus
    b. moodiness
    c. nausea in the early months
    d. toxemia
    e. fatigue

5. Stress among pregnant women

    a. affects fetal development in known, documented ways
    b. has been studied experimentally
    c. results in chemical changes in the woman's bloodstream
    d. a and c only
    e. b and c only

6. Which of the following problems are NOT associated with maternal diabetes?

    a. miscarriage
    b. stillbirth
    c. mental retardation of the fetus
    d. overweight of the baby
    e. all of the above are associated with maternal diabetes

7. Which of the following statements about nutrition and pregnancy is TRUE?

   a. a woman's caloric needs increase about 50% during pregnancy
   b. children conceived during the spring and summer are healthiest due to better maternal nutrition during those months
   c. infants born of malnourished mothers lag in motor and neurological development
   d. pregnant women need about 3000 calories a day
   e. all of the above

8. Parity

   a. refers to a woman's age when she bears a child
   b. affects the course of pregnancy and prenatal development
   c. refers to the number of previous children a woman has had
   d. a and b only
   e. b and c only

9. Alcohol consumption while pregnant

   a. is harmless to the fetus if ingested by the mother in small doses
   b. often results in lower fetal birth weight
   c. affects the fetus indirectly because it does not cross the placenta
   d. is most harmful during the first 3 months of pregnancy
   e. all of the above

10. The first stage of labor begins with uterine contractions and ends when

    a. the cervix is stretched to 4 inches
    b. the cervix is stretched to 10 inches
    c. the afterbirth is pushed out
    d. the baby is pushed through the birth canal
    e. the umbilical cord is cut

MATCHING

Match each statement with the letter corresponding to the period of pregnancy in which it occurs.

_____ 1. stomach and esophagus form
_____ 2. lanugo begins to grow over the body
_____ 3. fetus digests amniotic fluid and secretes urine
_____ 4. eyelids first open
_____ 5. vernix covers the body
_____ 6. blastocyst implants itself in the uterine wall
_____ 7. nerves form connections between brain, nose, and eyes
_____ 8. reflexive kicking movements start
_____ 9. cells of the embryo organize into functional units
_____ 10. organs are mature enough for 50 percent survival rate
      outside of the womb
_____ 11. brain can regulate breathing, body temperature,
      swallowing
_____ 12. intestines descend into the abdomen
_____ 13. finger and foot prints form
_____ 14. nerves cells begin to function
_____ 15. learning is possible

a. germinal stage
b. third and fourth weeks
c. second month
d. third month
e. fourth month
f. fifth month
g. sixth month
h. seventh month
i. eighth month
j. ninth month

ANSWERS TO THE SELF-TEST, CHAPTER 4

COMPLETION QUESTIONS

1. germinal (p. 81)
2. cephalocaudal (p. 83)
3. Fetology (p. 86)
4. self-righting (p. 96)
5. Thalidomide; phocomelia (p. 93)
6. 48; 12; 24 (p. 78)
7. pelvic inflammatory (p. 78)
8. 40 (p. 78)
9. umbilical cord (p. 82)
10. Teratology (p. 93)

MULTIPLE CHOICE

1. e (p. 77)
2. b (pp. 78-80)
3. d (pp. 81-82)
4. d (pp. 87-89)
5. c (p. 90)
6. c (p. 90)
7. c (pp. 91-92)
8. e (pp. 92-93)
9. b (p. 95)
10. a (p. 98)

MATCHING

1. c (p. 84)
2. f (p. 85)
3. d (pp. 84-85)
4. g (pp. 85-86)
5. f (p. 85)
6. a (pp. 81-82)
7. c (p. 84)
8. d (pp. 84-85)
9. b (pp. 82-84)
10. h (p. 86)
11. h (p. 86)
12. g (pp. 85-86)
13. e (p. 85)
14. i (pp. 86-87)
15. i (pp. 86-87)

CHAPTER SUMMARY

Chapter 5 outlines <u>physical and perceptual development</u> from birth to about two years. Tasks infants must master are noted, followed by a discussion of the most common risks infants face. A child's physical growth, including motor milestones and reflexes, is described, and sensory and perceptual abilities are discussed.

Birth is a stressful experience. An infant moves from the uterus to a world where breathing and feeding are no longer automatic. The Apgar test, given 1 and 5 minutes after birth, assesses the baby's condition. <u>Tasks for the newborn</u> include breathing, feeding, blood circulation, and temperature stabilization.

<u>Risks to infants</u> discusses four special risks children face in their first year. Premature birth, the most common birth complication, is most likely to occur in mothers who are young, in poor health, or are poorly nourished; who smoke, take drugs, are prone to infections, or have not had prenatal care. Many preterm babies survive, largely due to quality medical care, although 25% have moderately severe to very serious problems. Boys are more vulnerable to problems associated with prematurity. <u>Low birth weight</u> results from many of the same factors associated with prematurity. Many low birth weight babies have lower than average intelligence, and are vulnerable to other risks. Environmental conditions affect the subsequent development of low birth weight children. <u>Malnutrition</u> may result from inadequate prenatal maternal nutrition and lack of nutrients after birth. Breast feeding is an important predictor of infants' growth and health. Failure to thrive occurs when infants stop growing, lose weight, and lag behind in developmental milestones. No organic cause is apparent; infants may fail to thrive when they are ignored or their activities are restricted.

<u>Physical growth</u> details growth in the brain and body. An infants' environment has very little effect on brain growth. The sensorimotor cortex, brain stem, and cerebellum are the most active parts of the brain during the first month. Activity in the cerebral cortex is common by 4 months. <u>Body growth</u> is also primarily influenced by biological factors, including sex and birth order. A mother's size (her height, frame, and size of uterus) restrains the size of the fetus, although infants may catch up in size after birth.

<u>Reflexes of the newborn</u> describes some of the 20 reflexes of a healthy child. The rooting and sucking reflexes are necessary for survival. Other important reflexes are the palmar grasp, the moro reflex, the stepping reflex, and the tonic neck reflex.

<u>Infant states</u> over a 24 hour period are largely determined by

the central nervous system, and include sleep (66%), drowsiness (8%), fussiness (11%), alertness (10%), and crying (5%).

Motor development charts the motor milestones children achieve in their first two years. Age ranges when milestones are achieved are consistent across children. From birth to 3 months children can turn their heads, lift their chins, and at 2 to 3 months can keep their heads upright. During 4 to 6 months infants learn to roll from stomach to sides, roll onto their backs, grasp and hold items, and coordinate posture and gaze with the movements of their arms and hands. During 7 to 9 months infants roll from their backs to their stomachs, pull themselves up to standing, stand by holding on to something, shift toys from hand to hand, and crawl, creep, scoot, or walk. At 10 to 11 months infants can move from sitting to lying and back, and can walk by holding on to something. By age one, children can walk alone. There are variations in development that are influenced by both heredity and opportunity. Knowing motor milestones helps to spot children who are lagging behind -- which may signal problems.

Sensory and perceptual abilities describes changes in sensory perception. Infants' senses are less developed than adults'. At birth, an infant's vision is not sharp, but improves greatly in the first year. Infants prefer to look at patterns, especially those with curved contours, and a moderate amount of complexity and movement. Sensitivity and distance cues develop during the first six months. As with vision, infants do not hear as well as adults. Infants can discriminate between loud and soft and high and low sounds, and prefer human speech over other sounds. Baby talk is especially preferable. Infants can coordinate sight and hearing. Infants prefer the taste of sweet solutions over salty or bitter solutions. They can discriminate smells.

Finally, Perceptual processes discusses how infants come to know about their world. Exploration involves attending to the environment and selecting features to focus upon. Exploration increases with age. Children learn about events, objects and places by recognizing those things which remain constant -- invariants. Ability to perceive invariants improves with physical maturity and experience. Infants also learn what they can do with objects and what they can expect from them by perceiving object affordances.

LEARNING OBJECTIVES

When you have finished studying Chapter 5 in both the text and this guide, you should be able to do the following:

1.   State what the Apgar test is and what information it gives physicians.

2.   Identify changes the infant must adapt to in moving from the uterus to the outside world.

3.   Describe characteristics, causes, and treatments or prevention of prematurity, low birth weight, malnutrition, and failure to thrive.

4.   Describe how changes in brain growth during the first year relate to infants' abilities to interact with the world.

5.   List maternal and biological factors affecting body size and growth.

6.   Identify the types and usefulness of infant reflexes.

7.   Describe how infants spend their time, why sleep is important, and how sleep patterns change during the first year.

8.   Identify the sequence of motor development and the major motor milestones children achieve from birth to year one and onward.

9.   Relate how sensory development, in a general sense, influences perception.

10. List methods used to assess sensory capabilities.

11. Describe what an infant's visual capabilities and preferences are, and how these change during the first year.

12. Identify characteristics of the infant's auditory system that affect hearing, and preferences for particular sounds.

13. Discuss how infants use their senses to pick up information, and how this changes over time.

14. State what the concepts of invariants and affordances mean in Gibson's theory.

KEY TERMS

Apgar test (p. 108)

Full-term babies (p. 110)

INFANCY

Preterm babies (p. 110)

Postterm babies (p. 110)

Incubators (p. 111)

Small for gestational age (small for dates) (p. 113)

Marasmus (p. 113)

Colostrum (p. 115)

Failure to thrive (p. 115)

Restraining effect (p. 116)

Catch-up growth (p. 116)

Reflex (p. 117)

Rooting reflex (p. 117)

Sucking reflex (p. 117)

Palmar grasp (p. 119)

Moro (embracing) reflex (p. 119)

Stepping reflex (p. 119)

Myelination (p. 121)

Tonic neck reflex (p. 122)

Habituation (p. 126)

Retina (p. 126)

Fovea (p. 126)

Dendrites (p. 126)

Saccadic eye movements (p. 126)

Astigmatism (p. 127)

Accommodate (p. 127)

Depth of focus (p. 127)

Visual acuity (p. 127)

INFANCY

Visual cliff (p. 130)

Tympanum (p. 131)

Cochlea (p. 131)

Phoneme (p. 132)

Baby talk (p. 132)

Invariants (p. 136)

Shape constancy (p. 136)

Affordances (p. 136)

STUDY QUESTIONS

1. How has infant hospital care become more humanized? What effects have resulted from these efforts? (pp. 111-112)

2. What are some factors contributing to premature births, and how might prematurity be prevented? (pp. 110-111)

3. Both mothers and infants derive advantages from breast feeding. Describe some of these advantages. (pp. 113-115)

4. How does infant brain activity change in the first year? (pp. 115-116)

5. How does myelination relate to the acquisition of motor abilities? (p. 121)

6. What impact does practice and encouragement have on the development of motor abilities? (pp. 124-125)

7. Discuss the problems of assessing infants' sensory abilities, and some of the solutions researchers have devised to overcome these problems. (pp. 125-126)

INFANCY

8.   Compare the anatomy, physiology and functioning of
      infants' and adults' visual systems. (pp. 126-128)

9.   How does infants' hearing differ from adults' hearing?
      Explain the causes of these differences. (pp. 131-133)

10.   How do infants explore their environment? How does infant
      exploration change with age. (pp. 134-136)

11.   Infants are able to recognize objects and their
      usefulness. How do the Gibsons account for these
      perceptual abilities in infants? (pp. 136-137)

SELF-TEST, CHAPTER 5

COMPLETION QUESTIONS

1. Full term babies who are underweight are called _____.

2. _____ is a form of starvation in which infants barely grow, muscles atrophy, and if the infants survive they are unresponsive.

3. _____ is a term used to describe infants who stop growing and fall behind in reaching developmental milestones, yet no organic cause is responsible.

4. Two reflexes that help an infant to feed are the _____ reflex and the _____ reflex.

5. Infants are able to distinguish _____, _____, and _____ from milk.

6. Infants' ability to discriminate certain speech sounds is probably _____.

7. Infants most likely develop abilities to perceive distance during the first _____ months of life.

8. Infants may focus on contrast to keep the _____ of the visual cortex firing at a high level.

9. Rapid eye movements between one point of visual fixation and another are called _____ _____ _____.

MULTIPLE CHOICE

1. Which of the following is NOT scored in the Apgar test?

   a. heart rate
   b. respiration
   c. head size
   d. color
   e. reflex irritability

2. Which of the following do NOT generally occur immediately after birth?

   a. blood flow changes direction
   b. air sacs in the lungs inflate
   c. body temperature falls
   d. blood pressure rises
   e. all of the above occur

INFANCY

3. Which of the following statements concerning premature birth is FALSE?

    a. girls are more vulnerable to problems associated with prematurity than are boys
    b. 75% of premature babies have no serious problems if they have good hospital care
    c. premature infants tend to be more delayed in early motor development compared to full term infants
    d. IQ scores of premature infants tend to be lower than those of full term infants
    e. poorly nourished mothers are more likely than well nourished mothers to have premature children

4. Which of the following statements concerning an infant's physical growth is TRUE?

    a. brain growth is more affected by environmental factors, while body growth is primarily affected by biological factors
    b. brain activity in the first month of life occurs primarily in the cerebral cortex
    c. first born children usually weigh more than later born children, but later born children grow faster after birth to catch up
    d. on average, children triple their birth weight by age one
    e. all of the above

5. Infants spend approximately _____ percent of their time in active and quiet sleep.

    a. 33
    b. 50
    c. 66
    d. 75
    e. 90

6. Which of the following is NOT related to deficiencies in infants' vision?

    a. astigmatism
    b. habituation
    c. convergence
    d. depth of focus
    e. no distinct fovea

7. Infants prefer looking at the following kinds of objects:

    a. large
    b. patterned
    c. high contrast
    d. close
    (e). all of the above

8. Baby talk

    a. confuses children
    b. is harmful to infants' language development
    c. is well understood by infants
    (d). is adapted to infants sensory capacities
    e. always rhymes

9. It is known that infants can coordinate the following senses:

    a. hearing and taste
    b. touch and smell
    (c). vision and hearing
    d. taste and vision
    e. none of the above

10. James and Eleanor Gibson proposed that

    a. infants construct their perceptions of objects by acting on them
    b. infants are born with information about objects
    c. perception does not improve as the infant ages
    d. infants can only perceive objects that never change
    (e) infants have strong perceptual capacities at birth

INFANCY

MATCHING

A. Match the following motor milestones with the developmental period in which they are <u>first</u> likely to appear.

_____ 1. walk alone
_____ 2. stand by holding on to the edge of a surface
_____ 3. display the tonic neck reflex
_____ 4. move from sitting to lying and back
_____ 5. sit unsupported for 10 minutes
_____ 6. roll to sides from stomach
_____ 7. grasp objects handed to him or her
_____ 8. coordinate posture and gaze with arm and hand
           movements
_____ 9. roll onto back
_____ 10. crawl

a. birth to 3 months
b. 4 to 6 months
c. 7 to 9 months
d. 10 to 11 months
e. 12 months or later

B. Mark the letter of the matching answer in the space provided beside each item.

_____ 1. measured by observing infants' reactions to different
           patterns
_____ 2. allows infants to recognize the same objects in
           different places and times
_____ 3. smallest unit of language
_____ 4. used to test infants'depth perception
_____ 5. allows infant to know how an object functions

a. visual cliff
b. phoneme
c. invariants
d. affordances
e. visual preferences

ANSWERS TO THE SELF-TEST, CHAPTER 5

COMPLETION QUESTIONS

1. small for gestational age or small for dates (p. 113)
2. marasmus (p. 113)
3. failure to thrive (p. 115)
4. rooting and sucking (p. 117)
5. water, sugar, salt (p. 134)
6. innate (p. 132)
7. six (p. 131)
8. neurons (p. 128)
9. saccadic eye movements (p. 126)

MULTIPLE CHOICE

1. c (p. 108)
2. d (p. 109)
3. a (pp. 110-111)
4. d (pp. 115-116)
5. c (p. 120)
6. b (pp. 126-128)
7. e (pp. 127-128)
8. d (pp. 132-133)
9. c (p. 134)
10. e (pp. 135-137)

MATCHING

A.

1. e (p. 124)
2. c (pp. 122-123)
3. a (pp. 121-122)
4. d (p. 123)
5. c (pp. 122-123)
6. b (p. 122)
7. a (pp. 121-122)
8. b (p. 122)
9. b (p. 122)
10. c (pp. 122-123)

B.

1. e (p. 128)
2. c (p. 136)
3. b (p. 132)
4. a (p. 130)
5. d (p. 136)

CHAPTER SUMMARY

Chapter 6 covers the <u>cognitive development</u> of a child from birth to about 2 years. Topics of this chapter include the processes of learning; infant memory -- what we know and how it is studied; sensorimotor intelligence -- Piaget's perspective and criticisms of his views; intelligence testing in infancy; language development; and how cognitive development can be stimulated with toys and by parents.

<u>Learning in infancy</u> reviews the processes by which learning takes place. Classical conditioning, a way of learning demonstrated by Pavlov and then Watson, does not work well for infants less than 2 to 3 months old. Operant conditioning, which involves reinforcement for behavior, is successful for conditioning reflexes only before age 3 months. Other behaviors such as smiling, cooing, looking, reaching, pressing, and touching can be conditioned at age 3 months and older.

<u>Memory</u> discusses both <u>methods of studying infants' memory</u> and the <u>phases and functions of memory</u> for infants. Strategies for studying infant memory include (1) showing infants pairs of patterns and monitoring gaze length, (2) monitoring habituation patterns, (3) examining retention of learned behaviors, and (4) observing spontaneous behavior. These strategies helped to identify the phases of infant memory. Phase 1 memory is dependent on neurological wiring, is thoughtless, and is sensory-based. Phase 2 memory, from about 3 months to 6 or 7 months, is more cognitive. Active exploration and control of attention characterize this phase. Memories for patterns and details last several weeks. Phase 3, marked by organization, categorization, and generalization of information, begins at about 8 to 10 months. These memory abilities affect interactions with people and objects in the infants' environment.

Piaget's thinking about infant intelligence is outlined in the section <u>Sensorimotor intelligence</u>, along with criticisms of his approach. Piaget believed that although infants could not consciously think about their world, they relied on schemes -- generalizations built on repeated experiences -- to process information. Schemes are modified via adaptation. Information is assimilated (taken in) or accommodated (schemes are changed). Different schemes are combined and integrated (organized). Conflict helps move a child from one stage of development to the next through a process termed equilibration. All children advance through 6 consecutive stages of development in the same order in their first 2 years. Each stage builds on the previous stage. Stage 1 (birth to 1 month) involves practicing and repeating reflexes. During stage 2 (1 to 4 months) children begin repeating actions for pleasure. They learn objects are distinct from themselves, but do not realize that objects are permanent.

INFANCY

Stage 3 (4 to 8 months) is characterized by a magical understanding of cause and effect, by actions designed to prolong interesting sights, and by a rudimentary knowledge of object permanence. More varied use of schemes, a more sophisticated understanding of cause and effect, and a developing sense of object permanence occur in stage 4 (8 to 12 months). Experimentation and inference of cause from effect are the hallmarks of stage 5 (12 to 18 months). During the finalsensorimotor stage, stage 6 (18 to 24 months), children have amature understanding of object permanence, can perform mental combinations as they invent solutions to problems, and understanding of cause and effect is not dependent on their immediate perceptions. Research suggests that Piaget underestimated infants' abilities due to his method of study. Evidence indicates that infants achieve object permanence as early as 9 months, and this profoundly affects their thinking.

Infant intelligence tests are based on the work of Gesell, and include tests of eye-hand coordination, fine and gross motor skills, language ability, and personal-social behavior. Infant intelligence tests are not very predictive of future IQ scores for several reasons. First, content of intelligence tests for infants and other age groups differs greatly. And second, infant intelligence progresses in spurts, therefore tests may underestimate development.

The section on Language charts the processes and challenges facing children as they learn to speak. Basic abilities precede an infants' first words. These include months of practicing (babbling) and listening to sounds, and understanding that words represent concepts. First words are coupled with gestures. These holophrases can mean an entire paragraph. Pronunciation is imperfect due to infants' limited speech sounds. Familiar objects, action words, simple adjectives, and social or functional expressions are the first words children use. Infants learn word meanings by induction. Overextension, using words to cover extra meanings, and underextension, using a word more narrowly than it is intended, are common among infants. Responsive parents affect infants' language development.

Toys and parents are two influences discussed in the final section Stimulating cognitive development. Having a variety of stimulating objects available to manipulate and experiment with can enhance cognitive development. Parents can foster intellectual growth by talking to their children, and by providing them with interesting toys. Innate differences such as sex and temperament affect parental responses to children.

LEARNING OBJECTIVES

When you have finished studying Chapter 6 in both the text and this guide, you should be able to do the following:

1. Describe the ways that infants learn, and how learning changes over the first year of life.

2. Explain the methods scientists use in studying infant memory.

3. Discuss how changes in infant memory capabilities affect infant actions.

4. Define the key concepts of Piaget's theory of sensorimotor intelligence.

5. Describe what occurs in each of the 6 stages of Piaget's sensorimotor period of development.

6. Discuss criticisms of Piaget's theory and cite evidence supporting counter views.

7. Identify key components of infant intelligence tests, and note why these tests are useful.

8. Describe how a child acquires language.

9. Explain the role of toys in stimulating cognitive development.

10. Explain the role of parents in stimulating cognitive development.

KEY TERMS

Conditioned stimulus (p. 142)

Unconditioned stimulus (p. 142)

Unconditioned response (p. 142)

Conditioned response (p. 142)

INFANCY

Encode (p. 146)

Sensorimotor period (p. 147)

Schemes (p. 147)

Adaptation (p. 148)

Accommodation (p. 148)

Assimilation (p. 148)

Organization (p. 148)

Equilibration (p. 148)

Circular reactions (primary, secondary, & tertiary) (pp. 149,152)

Object permanence (p. 149)

Magico-phenomenistic thinking (p. 150)

A not B phenomenon (p. 153)

Babbling (p. 157)

Holophrase (p. 158)

Overextend (p. 161)

Underextend (p. 161)

STUDY QUESTIONS

1. Infants learn in a variety of ways. Describe the processes by which infants learn, and how the learning process changes in the first year. (pp. 142-144)

2. Describe the 4 ways scientists study infant memory. What some advantages of each method? (pp. 144-145)

3. There are different phases of infant memory. How does an infant's memory change during the first year? What implications do these changes have for how infants act? (pp. 145-147)

4. Define schemes. Describe the mental processes, according to Piaget, that guide infants' development of schemes. (pp. 147-148)

INFANCY

5.   Chart Piaget's theory of sensorimotor intelligence. What
     did Piaget claim occurred in each of the 6 stages of
     the sensorimotor period? (pp. 148-153)

6.   Cite criticisms of Piaget's theory of sensorimotor
     intelligence. (pp. 153-154)

7.   What factors should be considered in the development of
     infant intelligence tests? How are infant IQ tests useful?
     (pp. 154-155)

8.   Discuss the process of language acquisition. What must
     precede a child's first words? What are some typical first
     words and how are they pronounced? How are words learned?
     (pp. 155-163)

9.   Cite some common errors infants make when first beginning
     to speak. (p. 161)

10. How might toys stimulate cognitive development?
    (pp. 163-164)

11. How might parents stimulate cognitive development?
    (pp. 164-166)

12. Why might educated mothers pay more attention to their
    children than less educated mothers? (p. 165)

13. What aspects of an infant's development are more strongly
    influenced by genetics compared with the environment?
    Support your response with research. (pp. 165-166)

INFANCY

COMPLETION QUESTIONS

1. _Classical conditioning_ conditioning involves pairing a conditioned and unconditioned stimulus to produce a conditioned response.

2. _operant conditng_ conditioning involves performing, then finding the consequences of the behavior rewarding, and therefore repeating it.

3. In getting used to a pattern, or _habituat_ to it, scientists assume that infants remember seeing it.

4. The first phase of infants' memories depend on neurological _buildup_.

5. _encoding_ is the process of putting impressions into short-term memory.

6. According to Piaget, the sensorimotor period lasts from birth to about _2_ years.

7. _adaptation_, _organizati_, and _equilibriatn_ are three mental processes that guide the infants development of schemes.

8. Actions that are initially reflexive, then are repeated for pleasure are termed _primary_ _circular_ reactions. Actions that extend beyond the baby's own body to other objects or persons and are used to prolong interesting sights are termed _Secondary_ _Circular_ reactions.

9. _babbling_ is the earliest speech-like sounds and infant will make.

10. Using words to cover extra meanings is called _overextn_; using words too narrowly is termed _underext_.

MULTIPLE CHOICE

1. In John Watson's classical conditioning experiment in which Albert was taught to fear the white rat, the white rat was:

    a. the unconditioned stimulus
    b. the conditioned stimulus
    c. the unconditioned response
    d. the conditioned response
    e. the association

2. Which of the following statements regarding infant learning is TRUE?

    a. there is strong evidence that infants under 2-3 months old can be classically conditioned
    b. it has been easier to demonstrate classical, versus instrumental, conditioning of infants
    c. reflexes of newborns cannot be conditioned
    d. a broad range of behavior can be modified after a child is 3 months old
    e. all of the above

3. Which of the following was NOT cited by the text as a strategy used to study infant memory:

    a. comparing infants' reactions to pairs of familiar and unfamiliar patterns
    b. comparing infants' reactions to objects with those of other primates (particularly chimps)
    c. examining the time it takes an infant to habituate to a pattern
    d. finding out how long infants retain a learned response
    e. observing what infants spontaneously recall

4. Phase 2 of infant memory

    a. depends on neurological wiring
    b. is primarily sensory, rather than cognitive
    c. begins at about 1 month of age
    d. involves active exploration of the world
    e. ends at about 1 year

5. Organization and categorization of information by infants

    a. takes place during phase 2 of memory
    b. begins to occur between 11 and 12 months
    c. is evidenced as early as 2 months of age
    d. is accompanied by generalizations across time and place
    e. a and d only

6. Which of the following statements about schemes is NOT TRUE?

    a. they are the most basic units of knowledge
    b. they are generalizations built from specific experiences that are repeated
    c. they are guided by the processes of adaptation and organization
    d. they depend on consistency -- consistent properties of objects and consistent reactions of people
    e. all of the above are true

7.   Tests of all but which of the following are generally
     included in infant intelligence tests?

     a. counting ability
     b. fine motor skills
     c. gross motor skills
     d. eye-hand coordination
     e. personal-social behavior

8.   Which of the following statements regarding holophrases is
     NOT TRUE?

     a. they are comprised of one-word utterances and gestures
     b. they take the place of sentences or paragraphs
     c. they precede babbling
     d. they require an understanding that words are symbols
     e. they begin to appear at about 1 year

9.   Cindy uses the word "car" to mean cars, trucks, buses,
     planes and strollers. This is an example of:

     a. a holophrase
     b. a phoneme
     c. overextension
     d. underextension
     e. magico-phenomenistic thinking

10. The best type of toys to stimulate cognitive development
     are those that are:

     a. responsive
     b. loud
     c. cuddly
     d. musical
     e. unbreakable

MATCHING

Match each phrase with the corresponding letter of the
sensorimotor stage in which it is most likely to appear.

_f_ 1. object permanence achieved
_c_ 2. beginnings of an understanding of object permanence
_a_ 3. practice and repetition of reflexes
_e_ 4. can infer cause from seeing its effect
_d_ 5. can coordinate means and ends
_b_ 6. primary circular reaction
_c_ 7. secondary circular reaction
_e_ 8. tertiary circular reaction
_f_ 9. can form mental representations of cause and effect
independent of immediate perceptions
_b_ 10. beginning of understanding that objects are separate
from themselves

a. Stage 1 (0-1 month)
b. Stage 2 (1-4 months)
c. Stage 3 (4-8 months)
d. Stage 4 (8-12 months)
e. Stage 5 (12-18 months)
f. Stage 6 (18-24 months)

ANSWERS TO THE SELF-TEST, CHAPTER 6

COMPLETION QUESTIONS

1. classical (p. 142)
2. operant or instrumental (p. 143)
3. habituating (p. 144)
4. wiring (p. 146)
5. encoding (p. 146)
6. 2 (p. 142)
7. adaptation; organization; equilibration (p. 148)
8. primary circular; secondary circular (p. 149)
9. Babbling (p. 157)
10. overextension; underextension (p. 161)

MULTIPLE CHOICE

1. b (p. 142)
2. d (p. 143)
3. b (pp. 144-145)
4. d (p. 146)
5. d (p. 146)
6. e (p. 147)
7. a (pp. 154-155)
8. c (pp. 155-159)
9. c (p. 161)
10. a (p. 164)

MATCHING

1. f (pp. 152-153)
2. c (pp. 149-150)
3. a (p. 149)
4. e (p. 152)
5. d (pp. 150-151)
6. b (p. 149)
7. c (pp. 149-150)
8. e (p. 152)
9. f (pp. 152-153)
10. b (p. 149)

CHAPTER SUMMARY

In this chapter the development of and changes in communication between infants and key people in their world are described.

Mutual gazing characterizes the first meeting of mother and child. High hormone levels intensify a mother's receptivity to her child. Bonds between mother and child deepen over the next few months into strong emotional ties. Mothers who do not form deep bonds with their children are more likely to abuse or neglect them. Mothers who have extra early contact with their children sometimes feel more competent. There are many other opportunities for bonding other than immediately after birth. Postpartum blues are common among new mothers and result from physical and psychological changes following birth. Social support, a mother's personality and expectations, and the infant's responsiveness all affect the mother's adjustment to the new baby.

Infant communication highlights the variety of ways young children communicate. "Babyness" -- the cute appeal babies have -- is a means of attracting needed nurturance. Gazing is one type of communication. At 3 months, infants can maintain eye contact with mothers and feelings of attachment deepen as a result. Vocalizing, another form of communication, is initially random. Soon, however, infants are imitating sounds and are synchronizing their babbling with parents' speech. Smiling and laughing are other forms of communication. At 1 month children smile in response to events in the outside world. At 3 months they smile at human faces and familiar objects. At 5 months, smiles appear after mastering a task. Crying is another very powerful means of communicating. Infants cry because they are hungry or cold, hear quick, sharp noises, or are overstimulated. At 4 to 6 months, they may cry if frustrated or in response to seeing a stranger. Crying is not good for infants.

The slow and gradual process of learning socially proscribed ways of expressing emotions begins during infancy. Labels for emotions are learned with language. Parents are the primary source of knowledge about feelings. Infants respond to differences in other people's emotional expressions, and they use information about other people's emotions to guide their own behavior. Emotional suppression is common among two year olds, but occurs as early as age one.

The change from infant as communicator to infant as social partner is an ongoing process. From birth, infants are drawn into a parent-infant system as parents project feelings and intentions onto the child. Mother-child turn taking in feeding and talking has been documented. At about a year, children can fill in the words during talking turn-taking.

INFANCY

There are individual differences in mothers and children. Some
mothers are skilled, others are not. Mothers who are young,
poor, or have problems feeding may be less good at interpreting
signals from their children, and are therefore at risk for
abusing or neglecting their infants. Skill at interpreting
infant signals can be taught. Infants may be easy or difficult.
Three broad patterns of temperament have been identified, and
appear to be stable over time.

Becoming attached is a central goal of development in the infant
period. This section describes theories of attachment, how
attachment is assessed, patterns of attachment, how attachments
are formed, and the significance of a secure attachment.
Attachments are lasting, loving ties to the most important people
in an infant's world. In the preattachment phase infants can be
comforted by anyone. When infants can differentiate between
familiar people and strangers, and respond differently to their
parents versus others (usually at 2 to 3 months), the
preattachment phase end and Phase 2, attachment-in-the-making
begins. At 6 to 7 months a child begins to stay close to one
familiar person, and an attachment is formed. During clear-cut
attachment, Phase 3, a child is attached to a specific person.
This is evidenced by distress when the person leaves. This phase
lasts until age 2 or 3. Attachments are not restricted to
mothers; they can include a variety of others in a child's life.
Several theories of attachment have been advanced. Freud and
Erikson each noted the importance of maternal attachment, and
social learning theorists discuss it in light of learning
principles. Bowlby provides the most persuasive description of
attachment, and suggests that a need for closeness is a set goal
that each infant strives for. Ainsworth suggests this goal for
closeness must be balanced with a wish to explore the
surroundings. Attachment is assessed using a measure called the
strange situation. Patterns of attachment include (1) secure,
(2) insecure-avoidant, and (3) insecure-ambivalent. Secure
attachments are best fostered by a loving relationship with the
same person which continues unbroken from birth through infancy
and childhood. The quality of caregiver-infant relationships are
most important. Caregivers who treat infants warmly, smile at
them, play happily with them, and hold and cuddle them often are
likely to have securely attached children. Angry, critical,
rejecting, and interfering mothers are likely to have insecure
and avoidant infants. Infant temperament affects attachment.
Infants prone to distress are more likely to develop resistant,
ambivalent attachments. Environmental circumstances also impact
attachments. In situations of poverty, chronic maternal stress,
lack of social support, and marital difficulties, infants are
likely to develop insecure attachments. The quality of attachment
is related to later social and emotional competence in children.
Children with insecure attachments are not necessarily doomed to
develop problems. Research has indicated that competence can be
modified.

A <u>father's behavior</u> is important to infant development. Fathers
and mothers behave differently with their children. For example,
fathers spend less time than mothers physically caring for their
children, and they play more roughly with them. Finally, it is
noted that infants respond differently to mothers and fathers.

LEARNING OBJECTIVES

When you have finished studying Chapter 7 in both the text and
this guide, you should be able to do the following:

1. Describe the bonding process that occurs between mothers
   and newborns.

2. Discuss social and environmental factors that promote or
   inhibit mother-child bonding.

3. Describe common post-birth responses by mothers, and the
   factors affecting such responses.

4. Identify the different forms of infant communication.

5. Explain how gazing, vocalizing, and smiling change over
   time.

6. Identify why infants cry, and what messages crying signals
   at different ages.

7. Discuss the differences in infant and adult emotional
   expression.

8. Explain how children come to learn about appropriate
   emotional expression.

9. Describe the process by which infants become partners
   in communication with significant others.

10. Discuss differences between skilled and unskilled mothers,
    and implications of these differences for infant health.

11. Identify three types of infant temperaments.

12. Explain the phases of the development of attachments.

13. Discuss prominent theories of attachment.

14. Explain how attachment is assessed, and the resulting
    patterns of attachment.

15. Describe how secure attachments are formed, and the
    significant of having a secure attachment.

INFANCY

16. Discuss the differential responses by fathers and mothers to their children.

Sensitive period (p. 171)

Bonding (p. 171)

Rooming in (p. 171)

Endogenous smiles (p. 175)

Exogenous smiles (p. 175)

Stranger anxiety (fear of strangers)(p. 177)

Social referencing (p. 181)

Microanalysis (p. 182)

Pseudodialogues (p. 183)

Attachment (p. 186)

Set goal (p. 188)

Strange situation (p. 189)

Secure attachment (p. 190)

Insecure-avoidant attachment (p. 190)

Insecure-ambivalent attachment (p. 190)

STUDY QUESTIONS

1. Bonding between mother and infant is very important.
   Describe the process of bonding, and environmental and
   social factors that promote or impede this process.
   (pp. 171-172)

2. Many new mothers experience mood swings after giving
   birth. What factors affect a mother's adjustment to her
   newborn? (p. 172)

3. Infants communicate in a number of ways, including gazing.
   Describe how infants' gazing changes in the first few
   months, and the impacts this has on the mother.
   (pp. 173-174)

4. What function does smiling serve, and how does smiling change during the first 6 months? (pp. 175-176)

5. Discuss why infants cry, how crying changes over time, and parental responses to crying. (pp. 176-179)

6. Explain how children learn to modulate and control their emotional expression. (pp. 179-181)

7. Describe the results of research on parent and infant turn-taking. (pp. 181-183)

8. What differentiates a skilled from an unskilled mother? How do these differences affect infant health? (pp. 183-184)

9.   Explain the differences between easy, difficult, and
     slow-to-warm-up babies. (p. 185)

10. Compare and contrast Bowlby's views of attachment with
     those of Freud, Erikson, and Ainsworth. (p. 188)

11. Describe the process by which an infant becomes attached,
     and how attachment is assessed. (pp. 186-190)

12. Describe the various patterns of attachment. Why is it
     so important that infants form secure attachments? What
     factors affect the formation of secure attachments?
     (pp. 190-194)

13. How do fathers and mothers interact differently with
     their children? How have changes in family structure
     affected father-child interactions? (pp. 194-197)

INFANCY

COMPLETION QUESTIONS

1. Klaus and Kennel suggested that the moments after birth are a _sensitive_ _period_ when mothers easily form emotional bonds with their infants.

2. At about the age of _6_ weeks, infants can focus on their mother's eyes; At about _3_ months, infants are able to maintain eye contact with their mothers.

3. Smiles not triggered by social stimulation are called _endogenous_ smiles; Smiles occurring in response to events in the outside world are called _exogenous_ smiles.

4. _Social_ _referencing_ refers to infants' use of information about other people's emotions to guide their own behavior.

5. _Ainsworth_ suggested that an infant's set goal of seeking closeness to the mother must be balanced against the set goal of wanting to explore the surroundings.

6. Attachment is measured via the _Strange_ _situation_ .

7. The _preattachment_ phase of attachment formation ends when babies can tell people apart and recognize the difference between familiar people and strangers.

8. During the _attachment in the making_ phase of attachment formation, familiar people can console the baby better than unfamiliar ones can.

9. The _goodness_ of _fit_ between an infant's temperament and caregiver expectations is more important than the actual temperament in predicting development.

10. Fathers play more _roughly_ with their children than do mothers.

MULTIPLE-CHOICE

1. If the early sensitive period for bonding between mothers and newborns is missed or disrupted

    a. strong emotional bonds cannot be formed
    (b). strong emotional bonds are still likely to be formed
    c. strong emotional bonds are only likely to be formed if the mother seeks therapy
    d. the infant may bond with a nurse or doctor instead
    e. the infant is sure to have problems later in life

2. Mothers most readily adapt to the birth of a new baby if

   a. they have the support of family and friends
   b. they are nurturant
   c. they really wanted the baby
   d. their babies are responsive
   e. all of the above

3. By the age of _____ infants smile when they see a human face, doll, or other familiar object.

   a. 2 weeks
   b. 1 month
   c. 2 months
   d. 3 months
   e. 6 months

4. Crying caused by stranger anxiety may be qualitatively different from crying caused by pain because

   a. it is an immediate reaction to an event
   b. it is louder and more intense
   c. it involves cognitive processing
   d. it can be conditioned
   e. it only occurs after a child is about a year old

5. Children probably learn the most about feelings from

   a. their peers
   b. their parents
   c. their babysitters
   d. their teachers
   e. their siblings

6. Infants are able to "speak their own parts" in dialogues with their parents at about what age?

   a. 3 months
   b. 6 months
   c. 9 months
   d. 12 months
   e. 18 months

7. Mothers "at risk" for abusing their children

   a. may not be as adept at interpreting infants' emotional expression as other mothers
   b. tend to have children later in life
   c. can be helped professionally
   d. a and c only
   e. a, b, and c

8. Babies with slow-to-warm-up temperaments

   a. sleep and eat at the same time each day
   b. cry the most of any temperament type
   c. tend to have depressed moods
   d. take a while to adjust to new people and places
   e. do not react to small discomforts or frustrations

9. Babies with a(n) _____ attachment ignore or look away from their mothers when she returns to the room after the separation.

   a. secure
   b. insecure-avoidant
   c. insecure-ambivalent
   d. clear-cut
   e. non-

10. Which of the following statements about infants with insecure attachments is TRUE?

    a. insecurely attached infants are likely to have caregivers who treat them warmly and affectionately
    b. insecurely attached infants are likely to have mothers who are frequently angry with them
    c. insecurely attached infants tend to have slow-to-warm-up temperaments
    d. insecurely attached infants have sensitive, empathic mothers
    e. insecurely attached infants are likely to result from parents with good marriages

MATCHING

A. Match each statement with the letter of the corresponding theorist below.

_d_ 1. said attachment established the first and strongest love object

_c_ 2. discussed attachment in the context of the crisis between trust and mistrust

_f_ 3. focused on attachment as a secondary drive

_b_ 4. called attachment a set goal

_a_ 5. said the need for closeness must be balanced against the need to explore the surroundings

a. Mary Ainsworth
b. John Bowlby
c. Eric Erikson
d. Sigmund Freud
e. Ivan Pavlov
f. social learning theorists
g. John Watson

B. Match each statement with the corresponding letter below.

_g_ 1. used to increase contact between mother and newborn

_a_ 2. attracts nurturance and helps to insure survival

_e_ 3. used to understand parent-child communication

_c_ 4. the most common temperament type identified by Thomas and Chess

_f_ 5. turn taking between parent and child in which the parent "fills in the parts" for the child

a. babyness
b. difficult
c. easy
d. Lamaze method
e. microanalysis
f. pseudodialogues
g. rooming in
h. slow-to-warm-up
i. vocalization

ANSWERS TO THE SELF-TEST, CHAPTER 7

COMPLETION QUESTIONS

1. sensitive period (p. 171)
2. 6; 3 (pp. 173-174)
3. endogenous; exogenous (p. 175)
4. Social referencing (p. 181)
5. Ainsworth (p. 188)
6. strange situation (p. 189)
7. preattachment (p. 186)
8. attachment-in-the-making (p. 187)
9. goodness-of-fit (p. 187)
10. roughly or physically (p. 195)

MULTIPLE-CHOICE

1. b (pp. 171-172)
2. e (p. 172)
3. d (p. 175)
4. c (p. 177)
5. b (p. 180)
6. d (p. 183)
7. d (p. 184)
8. d (p. 185)
9. b (p. 190)
10. b (pp. 190-194)

MATCHING

A.

1. d (p. 188)
2. c (p. 188)
3. f (p. 188)
4. b (p. 188)
5. a (p. 188)

B.

1. g (p. 171)
2. a (p. 173)
3. e (p. 182.)
4. c (p. 185)
5. f (p. 183)

CHAPTER SUMMARY

The section Physical growth is subdivided according to patterns of growth, changes in physical size and proportion, and factors that influence growth. Constant changes in growth patterns are the result of cell and organ development in the body. Growth in this period, as in infancy, is asynchronous: organs and other body parts grow at different rates. Cell growth occurs in one of three ways, depending on the type of cell. The internal growth patterns produce highly visible external changes in children's height and weight. Growth curves chart these changes and can be used to develop norms of growth for subgroups of children. If a child is far outside the norms of growth for his or her subgroup, this may indicate a problem that needs attention. Changing size and proportions illustrates the phenomenal rate of physical growth of preschoolers by presenting expected increases in weight and height for each year.

Factors affecting growth discusses the role of genetics, nutrition, parental neglect and emotional abuse in normal and abnormal physical growth in children. Genetic factors may explain abnormal growth, such as dwarfism and giantism, as well as the normally observed growth differences between boys and girls. Malnutrition, neglect and abuse can lead to many physical abnormalities. Nutrients are crucial during early childhood growth. Fortunately, interventions, such as changes in diet or surroundings, can sometimes reverse the adverse effects of malnutrition and neglect.

The section Brain growth covers four major topics: (1) determinants of brain growth and functioning; (2) brain structure and organization; (3) brain and behavior; and (4) brain lateralization. Brain growth and functioning depends mainly on properties and processes related to the development of nerve cells, and connections between them. Brain structure and organization describes the sequence and specifics of neuronal changes related to brain maturation. Neuronal growth, combined with other chemical and physical changes, re-structures the brain, making it more efficient, with a wider range of possible behaviors. Brain and behavior discusses the associations between brain maturation and advances in various children's behaviors. Brain lateralization explains that the cortex is divided into two hemispheres that each have specialized functions. Specialized functions by hemisphere are found in both adults and children, and are believed to develop in early infancy.

Physical abilities and changes indicates that children's repertoire of skills, and competence in performing them, increase according to a maturational timetable and life experiences. There is a typical sequence of skill development that follows from the maturational timetable: children's large motor skills (e.g., cycling, jumping, catching) improve before fine motor and perceptual skills (e.g., stringing beads or focusing on print). This section also notes that physiological changes in early childhood decrease children's vulnerability to sickness.

The final section, <u>Child abuse</u>, reports estimates of numbers of children whose physical well-being is damaged and threatened by their parents. The roots of child abuse are difficult to determine. Some researchers blame deficiencies in parents or children, while others suggest that some combination of parent and child factors results in abuse. Child abuse appears to be transmitted across generations, and recommendations are made for interventions.

LEARNING OBJECTIVES

When you have finished studying Chapter 8 in both the text and this guide, you should be able to do the following:

1. Discuss the major causes and patterns of physical growth and development in early childhood.

2. Explain how physicians and child specialists identify abnormalities in height and weight, and what these abnormalities signify.

3. Discuss how and why males and females differ in physical growth.

4. Explain the effects of genetic factors on growth.

5. Describe the symptoms, causes and effects of malnutrition and neglect.

6. Indicate what properties and processes determine brain development and function.

7. Note the major brain structures that develop in early childhood, and discuss how these structural changes affect brain functioning.

8. Explain how changes in brain size, complexity, and myelination may cause changes in behavior.

9. Define brain lateralization.

10. Discuss how physical abilities and health change with physical development.

11. Describe the "vicious cycle of child abuse."

KEY TERMS

Asynchrony (p. 204)

Growth curve (p. 204)

Dwarfism (p. 208)

Giantism (p. 208)

Kwashiorkor (p. 209)

Neurotransmitters (p. 211)

Neuroglia (p. 211)

Fissures (p. 211)

Nissl substance (p. 211)

Corpus callosum (p. 212)

Lateralization (p. 212)

Child abuse (p. 214)

STUDY QUESTIONS

1. Describe how cell growth affects organ growth, and the three ways that cells grow. (p. 204)

2. What is the value of charting the height and weight of children? (pp. 204-206)

3. Describe the changes in weight, height, and proportion of height during early childhood. (pp. 206-208)

4. How do genetic factors influence differences in physical growth and in the development of motor skills between boys and girls? (pp. 208-209)

5. How does malnutrition interfere with normal development? (pp. 209-210)

6.   How does severe emotional stress affect children's growth?
     (p. 210)

7.   Describe three major developments and changes related to
     neurons, or nerve cells, in the brain. (p. 211)

8.   Describe the development of neuroglia, myelin and fissures
     in the brain (p. 211).

9.   How does myelination relate to the acquisition of motor
     abilities? (p. 212)

10. What behaviors are thought to be governed by the brain's
     right and left hemispheres, respectively? (p. 212)

EARLY CHILDHOOD

11. Preschool children develop large and fine motor skills, as well as perceptual skills. Which of these skills develops fastest, and what does this development enable children to do? (p. 213)

12. What did Main and George discover when they compared a group of abused children and their mothers with a matched group of non-abused children and their mothers? (p. 216)

SELF-TEST, CHAPTER 8

COMPLETION QUESTIONS

1. _____ refers to the uneven growth rates of different organs, that is typical of how human beings grow both before and after birth.

2. A _____ _____ is a record of a child's pattern of physical change over time.

3. By age 2, a boy is about _____ his adult height, a girl is slightly more than _____ her adult height.

4. The brain's _____ gland follows genetic instructions that cause it to produce growth hormone and other hormones that affect growth.

5. Kwashiorkor, a form of severe malnutrition affecting children between 2 and 4 years, results from a _____ deficiency.

6. Children exposed to severe emotional distress are short and immature in _____ development.

7. _____ substance surrounds the cell nucleus of neurons, and often appears at the same time as a new behavioral function appears.

8. Increases in brain size, complexity, and myelination are related to advances in children's _____ , _____ and _____ .

9. The _____ _____ is a tough band of myelinated tissue that connects the two hemispheres of the cortex.

10. Motor skills develop according to a maturational timetable, but also depend upon _____ .

MULTIPLE CHOICE

1. Which of the following CANNOT be determined by growth curves?

    a. normal height of a 4-year-old American child
    b. abnormal growth rates
    c. normal weight of a 4-year-old girl
    d. changes in height from one age to the next
    e. how many diseases children have

EARLY CHILDHOOD

2.   Which of the following changes in growth does NOT generally occur?

a. gain 15 pounds and 10 inches in the first year of life
b. gain 5 pounds and 5 inches in the second year of life
c. gain 4.5 pounds and 4 inches in the third year of life
d. growth rate starts to slow down by age 3
e. none of the above

3.   Which of the following statements about differences between boys' and girls' physical development is TRUE?

a. newborn girls' fingers are thinner, allowing them to sew better than boys
b. newborn girls' skeletal systems are several weeks more mature than newborn boys'
c. newborn boys' permanent teeth grow in sooner than girls' do
d. by adolescence, boys' skeletal systems are the same size as girls' are
e. newborn boys suffer from dwarfism, while girls do not

4.   A study of children in Swedish cities showed no connection between children's height and family income, presumably because in Sweden:

a. all preschoolers receive hormone therapy
b. wealthy people invite poor children to dine with them
c. poor children live in foster homes
d. poor and rich alike have access to food and social services
e. severe droughts create dietary deficiencies for rich and poor people

5.   Which of the following is the LEAST important to the development of the brain and behavior?

a. size of the mother's birth canal
b. covering of myelin on the nerve cells
c. elimination of redundant or inefficient nerve connections
d. branching dendrites at the ends of the nerve cells
e. number, size, and structure of neurons

6. Which of the following statements about physical abilities and changes is FALSE?

   a. children vary widely in their fine motor skills
   b. play exercises and develops muscles, senses, and coordination
   c. average body temperature of a 1-year-old is 10 degrees Fahrenheit higher than that of the average 5-year-old
   d. after the age of 2, children's heart and breathing rates slow; average body temperature falls, and fevers get lower
   e. preschoolers are less vulnerable to infections than infants

7. Parents who abuse their children:

   a. often brag about hitting children
   b. feel personally inadequate and have low self-esteem
   c. want to be caught
   d. are likely to be impatient, immature, and know little of child development
   e. b and d only

MATCHING

A. Match the following statements about child growth with the developmental period in which they are first likely to appear.

_____ 1. head is one-fourth of body size
___e___ 2. children are about 70 percent of their adult height
_____ 3. arms and legs grow more quickly than the body
_____ 4. most baby fat is lost
_____ 5. muscle and bone growth quickens

a. newborn
b. end of first year
c. after first year
d. 2 to 3 years
e. by age 6

EARLY CHILDHOOD

B. Mark the letter of the matching answer in the space provided beside each statement about physical development.

_____d__ 1. bloated bellies, thin and colorless hair, skin lesions
_____a__ 2. white fatty substance that improves the transmission of signals along the neurons
_____b__ 3. develop as the neurons enlarge and are myelinated
_____e__ 4. pedal a tricycle, catch a ball, climb a ladder
_____c__ 5. hold a pencil and focus on a line of print

a. myelin
b. fissures
c. fine motor and perceptual skills
d. characteristics of kwashiorkor
e. large motor skills
f. dwarfism

ANSWERS TO THE SELF-TEST, CHAPTER 8

COMPLETION QUESTIONS

1. asynchrony (p. 204)
2. growth curve (p. 204)
3. half, half (p. 208)
4. pituitary (p. 208)
5. protein (p. 209)
6. bone (p. 210)
7. Nissl (p. 211)
8. thinking, acting, talking (p. 212)
9. corpus callosum (p. 212)
10. experience (p. 213)

MULTIPLE CHOICE

1. e (pp. 204-206)
2. e (pp. 206-207)
3. b (pp. 208-209)
4. d (p. 210)
5. a (pp. 211-212)
6. c (pp. 213-214)
7. e (pp. 214-216)

MATCHING

A.

1. a (p. 208)
2. e (p. 208)
3. c (p. 208)
4. d (p. 208)
5. b (p. 208)

B.

1. d (pp. 209-213)
2. a (pp. 209-213)
3. b (pp. 209-213)
4. e (pp. 209-213)
5. c (pp. 209-213)

CHAPTER SUMMARY

Symbolic thought describes children's use of symbols to represent objects and actions in fantasy play, drawing and speaking. Symbolic thought, according to Piaget, emerges in the years from 1 to 4. Fantasy play shows early evidence of children's developing symbolic thought. Children in this age period may not be able to separate fantasy from reality, and they may use symbolic play to cope with fears or learn new behaviors. Symbolic play changes as children mature; symbolic play with objects changes to pretend play, which evolves into dramatic play. Drawing is another representation of children's symbolic thought capacities. The nature of children's drawings may reflect their mental images of the world, or their physical inability to adequately depict what they imagine. Words are perhaps the most important form of symbolic representation, since they can be used to understand the connection between language and objects, events and relationships.

Intuitive thought is present in 4- to 6-year-old children, while fantasy is more common among 2- and 3-year-olds. The intuitive process is evident in children's somewhat immature reasoning about reality. Dreams are interpreted by children according to their intuition, and the interpretations appear to change in stages as children grow older. Animism is another characteristic of intuitive thought. Children have difficulty distinguishing living from non-living things, and they believe that non-living things have feelings, intentions and thoughts. There is some evidence that children can make adequate distinctions between animate and inanimate things once they have been educated about these differences. Perspective taking is a quality of intuitive thought that reflects children's egocentrism. The ability to take the perspective, or view, of another increases throughout the early childhood years.

The section Preoperational logic describes the state of children's cognitive processes before they are able to perform logical operations like addition and multiplication. Piaget calls the stage of preoperational logic the preoperational period. Evidence of preoperational logic is found in children's reasoning and conservation abilities. Transductive reasoning (i.e., reasoning from one particular to another rather than from the general to the particular) is one expression of preoperational logic. There is some controversy over young children's ability to think deductively. For example, there is evidence that children can reason adequately about cause and effect, especially when asked about things they are familiar with. Another form of preoperational logic is evident in children's inability conserve, or know that outward changes in an object's appearance (e.g., how it is arranged) does not mean its length, quantity, mass, area, weight and volume also change.

EARLY CHILDHOOD

Cognitive development is thought to occur in stages. Following the preoperational logic period, children enter a stage of transition before they can perform logical operations. Piaget holds that all children transition across these three phases -preoperational to transitional to operational - in all domains (e.g., conservation for numbers should be similar to conservation of volume). Shifts from one stage to the next are relatively sudden (i.e., discontinuous), and irreversible.

The information processing approach is an alternative to Piaget's framework for describing preschool children's thinking. This approach emphasizes quantitative rather than qualitative changes in children's abilities. Two central factors in children's thinking, or "information processing," are attention and memory. In order for children to process information they must attend to information in their environment. Future use of information depends on children's ability to retrieve, or remember, the information. As children mature, they are better able to selectively attend to and remember important aspects of their environment.

The section Language explains that preschool children's rapidly expanding vocabulary is dependent upon their syntactical framework. The development of syntax (e.g., how words are combined into sentences for expression) begins with one-word utterances. Next, children speak in concise, two-word telegraphic "sentences." Increasingly complex sentences emerge slowly, and are characterized by errors in verb tenses and plurals (overregularization). The speed and level of language development depends on both innate ability and environmental input. Various theories discuss the relative contributions of natural and environmental influences on the development of speech. Parents are thought to influence language development by attending to children's messages and responding to them. Parent's also tend to "gauge" their responses to the child's level of language understanding.

The context of cognitive development is organized according to four important environmental factors -- toys, television, parents, programs -- that affect children's cognitive development in early childhood. These four factors influence the kind and amount of stimulation and attention a child's environment provides. The kind of stimulation is very important. For example, not all children viewing television demonstrate cognitive advances, but children watching Sesame Street do. Quality of stimulation is also important for children attending preschool enrichment programs, such as Head Start. Programs that have an educational component appear to be beneficial to children's cognitive development.

LEARNING OBJECTIVES

When you have finished studying Chapter 9 in both the text and this guide, you should be able to do the following:

1. Discuss how children use symbols to represent objects and actions while engaged in symbolic play and drawing, and in their use of words.

2. Describe the characteristics of children's drawings, and what their drawings indicate about their underlying mental representations.

3. Discuss developmental changes in word acquisition, and the importance of symbolic thought for proper word usage.

4. Describe intuitive thought, and discuss how dreams and animistic thinking reflect intuitive thought.

5. Indicate the relation of egocentrism to perspective taking abilities, and how children demonstrate egocentrism.

6. List the major characteristics of thinking of children in the preoperational period of cognitive development.

7. Define and give examples of transductive reasoning.

8. Describe conservation and how it is demonstrated in children's problem solving behaviors (i.e., reversibility, reciprocity, and decentration).

9. Discuss the developmental stages Piaget observed for conservation and seriation in all domains of children's thinking.

10. List the important components of information processing theory, and discuss how this theory departs from Piaget's stage theory.

11. Explain how language development results from both innate abilities and environmental input.

12. Explain how cognitive development is affected by toys, television, parents, home environment, and preschool programs.

13. Discuss the meaning of the phrase "critical period."

EARLY CHILDHOOD

KEY TERMS

Symbol (p. 220)

Symbolic play (p. 220)

Intuition (p. 222)

Animism (p. 223)

Egocentrism (p. 224)

Operations (p. 226)

Preoperational period (p. 226)

Transductive reasoning (p. 226)

Conservation (p. 228)

Reversibility (p. 229)

Reciprocity (p. 229)

Decentration (p. 229)

Horizontal decalage (p. 231)

Recognition (p. 236)

Recall (p. 236)

Syntax (p. 239)

Telegraphic sentence (p. 239)

Overregularize (p. 240)

Motherese (p. 243)

Head start (p. 250)

Nursery school (p. 252)

STUDY QUESTIONS

1. What behaviors are possible with the advent of symbolic
    thinking? Describe three major ways that children show
    their symbolic thinking abilities. (pp. 220-222)

2. According to Erik Erikson, what is the role of symbolic play in childhood? (p. 221)

3. Starting with Piaget, discuss the competing theories about deficiencies in children's drawing. (pp. 221-222)

4. How does intuition influence children's interpretations of dreams and beliefs about inanimate objects? (pp. 223-224)

5. How do researchers test perspective taking abilities? (pp. 224-225)

6. According to Piaget, what cognitive limitations do children have in the preoperational period? Focus discussion on logical operations, reasoning processes, and conservation. (pp. 225-231)

7. Discuss the five traditional methods of testing children's abilities to conserve length, liquid quantity, substance amount, area, and volume. (p. 230)

8. What are the major assumptions and problems underlying Piaget's three stages of cognitive development --preoperational, transitional, and operational. (pp. 231-234)

9. Compare the attention capacities of preschoolers with older children. (pp. 234-236)

10. What is the difference between recognition and recall? (pp. 236-237)

11. Describe the sequence of language development. (pp. 237-245)

13. How do innate abilities constrain language development?
    (pp. 245-246)

14. Discuss several important environmental factors that affect
    preschooler's cognitive development. (pp. 246-252)

15. What evidence is there that many early childhood experiences
    are reversible, as opposed to critical and permanent?
    (p. 251)

SELF-TEST, CHAPTER 9

COMPLETION QUESTIONS

1. According to Piaget, symbolic thought is a cognitive activity that emerges in the years from __1__ to 4.

2. Pretending a tin-can is a phone is an example of the simplest kind of fantasy play, called _Symbolic_ play.

3. Between the ages of 1 and 4, children's fantasy play progresses from symbolic play with objects, to _pretend_ play in which they act like grown-ups, and finally to _dramatic_ play with roles announced ahead of time.

4. Some developmental psychologists have suggested that children omit details from their drawings because their _memory_ or their physical abilities are limited.

5. Children usually have acquired their first recognizable words by their __1__ birthday.

6. _Intuitive_ thought is common among 4-, 5-, and 6-year-old children, and is characterized by guesses about reality rather than rational inferences.

7. Around the age of 4 years children think that dreams are real events that happen outside of themselves; by the age of __5__ or __6__ years they understand that dreams come from inside a person's head but think they happen outside of it; by the time they are about __7__ years old they clearly understand that dreams are thoughts and imaginings that come from within a person.

8. The belief that inanimate things are living and have feelings, intentions, and thoughts just as humans do is called _animism_ .

9. Research on perspective taking suggests that young children are limited by their ability to perform mental _operations_ (like rotating a scene in their minds) rather than that they simply do not realize that other people have perspectives that are different from their own.

10. Children in the period of early childhood cannot perform logical operations, like _+_ , _X_ , _−_ which transform information and form an organized network of knowledge.

11. Reasoning from one particular to another rather than from the general to the particular is called _transductive_ reasoning.

12. _Conserv___ is the name given to the understanding that even though an object's outward appearance may change, its length, quantity, mass, area, weight, and volume do not change as well.

13. Piaget observed that children acquire conservation of different quantities at different ages. He called this phenomenon _horizontal_ _decalage_ .

14. The information processing approach to studying children's thinking emphasizes _gradual_ changes in children's abilities, not stages.

15. Children's first sentences are very basic and terse. Such speech includes sentences such as "Mommy give" or "Doggy bark," which are called _telegraphic_ sentences.

16. Young children seek general rules of language that operate consistently. When they encounter irregular verbs or plurals they tend to _over regularize_ these words, by tacking -ed or -s onto the end of them.

17. B.F. Skinner suggested that children learn language as adults systematically _reinforce_ their efforts; while Noam Chomsky suggested that much of children's language capacity is _innate_

MULTIPLE CHOICE

1. Which of the following is NOT evidence of the development of symbolic thought capacities in young children?

   a. pretending to be an animal
   b. talking to an imaginary playmate
   c. difficulty separating fantasy from reality
   d. pushing your mother down the stairs
   e. acting like a grown-up

2. Which of the following statements about intuitive thought is FALSE?

   a. intuitive thinkers have difficulty separating real and imagined events
   b. intuitive thinkers understand that dreams are thoughts and imaginings that come from within a person
   c. intuitive thinkers believe that objects move because they want to
   d. all of the above
   e. none of the above

3. When a child is able to view a problem from another's pont-of-view, then he/she is demonstrating:

   a. conservation
   b. perspective-taking
   c. reciprocity
   d. recognition
   e. reversibility

4. Which of the following statements about children's reasoning is TRUE?

   a. young children reason from the general to the particular
   b. children younger than 4 have been known to reason deductively
   c. preschoolers understand that a physical cause precedes its effect
   d. young children understand that for something to be the cause of an event, it must *always* be followed by the event.
   e. only b and c

5. Which of the following statements about stage theories is TRUE?

   a. transitions between stages are gradual
   b. transitions between stages occur at exactly the same age for all children
   c. the operational stage of development occurs before the preoperational stage
   d. everyone achieves the highest stage of cognitive development by the end of the early childhood period
   e. none of the above

6. Indicate which 3 of the following qualitative changes seen on Piaget's tasks seem to differentiate the thinking of preschoolers and school-age children?

   a. preschool children depend on the appearance of things; while school-age children are sensitive to distinctions between what *seems* to be and what really *is*
   b. preschool children attend to less features than school-age children do
   c. preschool children do not understand reversibility; older children do
   d. preschool children cannot think deductively; older children can
   e. school-age children do not engage in pretend play; younger children do

7. Why do preschoolers remember less than school-age children
    and adults?

    a. they cannot pay attention to things
    b. they are less selective about information they attend to
    c. they are unable to recognize objects they have seen
    d. they have not developed recall abilities
    e. they do not have any memory strategies

8. Which of the following is NOT a part of language
    development?

    a. speaking in telegraphic sentences
    b. increased knowledge of syntax
    c. deregulation
    d. reinforcement
    e. imitation

9. Motherese:

    a. interferes with preschooler's language development
    b. occurs with the onset of pregnancy
    c. is the name of a famous Christian missionary who helps
       starving children
    d. consists of short simple sentences that may be repeated
       in different forms for emphasis
    e. is used by mothers, not fathers, when talking to their
       babies

10. Which of the following affects the cognitive development
    of children?

    a. the number and kinds of toys they play with
    b. the television shows they watch
    c. the stimulation they receive from parents and peers
    d. attending preschool educational programs
    e. all of the above

MATCHING

A. Match the following statements about word acquisition with
    the age in which they are first likely to appear.

    ___ 1. have vocabularies of 5-10,000 words
    ___ 2. acquire their first recognizable words
    ___ 3. words used are understood and reflect symbolic thought
    ___ 4. adding an average of five to seven new words each day

a. birth to 1 year
b. 1.5 to 2 years
c. 2 to 3 years
d. 5 years

B. Mark the letter of the matching answer in the space provided
    beside each statement about cognitive development.

_____ c   1. thought is marked by guesses about reality rather than
              rational inferences
_____ a   2. believing that inanimate objects have feelings
_____ d   3. cannot perform logical operations in this period
_____ e   4. understanding that dimensions like height and width or
              length and thickness are reciprocal or complementary
_____ b   5. research that focuses on how children attend
              to information in the environment and store that
              information in memory
_____ i   6. allow children to remember familiar events and routines
              by forming a general organizational framework of
              knowledge about those things
_____ g   7. how words are combined into sentences to express who
              did what to whom
_____ f   8. important contextual factors that affect cognitive
              development
_____ j   9. refers to the notion that early experience has
              permanent effects
_____ h   10. educational enrichment program

a. animism
b. information processing approach
c. intuition
d. preoperational period
e. reciprocity
f. toys, television, preschool educational programs
g. syntax
h. nursery school
i. scripts
j. critical period
k. transitioning
l. logical operations

ANSWERS TO THE SELF-TEST, CHAPTER 9

COMPLETION QUESTIONS

1. 1 (p. 220)
2. symbolic (p. 220)
3. pretend, dramatic (p. 221)
4. memories (p. 221-222)
5. first (p. 222)
6. intuitive (p. 222)
7. 5,6,7 (p. 223)
8. animism (p. 223)
9. operations (p. 225)
10. addition, multiplication, subtraction (p. 226)
11. transductive (p. 226)
12. conservation (p. 228)
13. horizontal decalage (p. 231)
14. quantitative (p. 234)
15. telegraphic (p. 239)
16. overregularize (p. 240)
17. reinforce, innate (p. 242)

MULTIPLE CHOICE

1. d (pp. 220-222)
2. b (pp. 222-224)
3. b (pp. 224-225)
4. e (pp. 226-228)
5. e (p. 231)
6. a,b,c (p. 233)
7. b (pp. 234-237)
8. c (pp. 239-246)
9. d (pp. 243-245)
10. e (pp. 246-252)

MATCHING

A.

1. d (p. 222)
2. a (p. 222)
3. c (p. 222)
4. b (p. 222)

B.

1. c (p. 222)
2. a (p. 223)
3. d (p. 226)
4. e (p. 229)
5. b (p. 234)
6. i (p. 237)
7. g (p. 239)
8. f (pp. 246-249)
9. j (p. 251)
10. h (p. 252)

CHAPTER SUMMARY

The section on <u>Relations with parents</u> describes how preschool
children become increasingly autonomous, yet maintain a steady
and healthy attachment to parents. Children express their
<u>developing autonomy</u> by acting less distressed when separated
from parents. Although older children tolerate longer periods
of separation from parents, their emotional attachment --secure,
withdrawn, ambivalent -- is stable between 1 and 6 years.

<u>Socialization and discipline</u> discusses various parenting styles
and consequences for children. In the preschool years parents
become more involved in socializing and disciplining their
children. Boundaries are set in response to children's
increasing expressions of autonomy, and standards of appropriate
behavior are taught. <u>Authoritarian parents</u> are firm, punitive,
and unsympathetic in their handling of children. This treatment
tends to create suspicion, withdrawal and discontent in
children. <u>Permissive parents</u> are lax about regulating
children's impulses and behaviors. Their children tend to be
immature, dependent and unhappy. <u>Authoritative parents</u> fall
somewhere in between the heavy-handedness of authoritarian
parents and the liberal style of permissive parents.
Authoritative parents strive to limit conflict, establish few
but firm rules, and reason with children. Their children are
most likely to be friendly, competent, independent, happy and
socially responsible. Recently, researchers also have asked how
children influence parents' disciplinary styles.

While direct methods, such as punishment or rewards, can alter
behaviors, children also learn simply by <u>observing</u> people in
action. Acting from memory, children can imitate a wide range
of behaviors depending on the situation.

The changing structure of modern families can both cause and
result from stress. <u>Family stressors</u> result from two important
factors in today's family landscape: divorce and maternal
employment. These factors have important implications for
preschool children's social and emotional development. Research
on <u>divorce</u> has shown that family relations tend to be erratic
for two years after the divorce, and children become unruly.
Boys, with the exception of those with father contact, present
more social problems than girls. The effects of divorce seem to
stem from changes in the continuity of family relationships, and
decreased tolerance levels of parents. <u>Mother's work</u> is another
potential source of stress for child and family. Daughters of
working mothers tend to benefit (e.g., they are more independent
and socially adjusted), while boys generally fare less well
(e.g., they are socially maladjusted and achieve less in
school). The root of these sex differences is not clear.

Another important element of preschoolers social development is

learning to get along with others. To start, many children
learn to develop social relationships with brothers and sisters.
Siblings can learn from each other through imitation, and rely
on each other for emotional support and comfort.

Children also establish social ties outside of the immediate
family. The section on Interactions with other children
explains the nature of these ties, by describing patterns of
peer play over the preschool period. Play patterns become more
sophisticated with age. For 2- and 3-year-olds play is mainly
parallel (e.g., playing beside, and not with a peer) and
ritualistic (e.g., repetitive, rhythmic exchanges or turns).
Toys are an important part of social interaction at this age.
Older preschoolers tend to engage in more positive play and
language play.

In social skills development, acts of sharing tend to precede
caring actions. Also, the discussion Sharing and caring
indicates that the emotional response of empathy for another's
distress is present by this age. Prosocial behaviors (e.g.,
offers of comfort) stemming from empathic responses become more
effective at later ages. Children can express antisocial
behaviors too, such as hitting and hurting. Aggressive,
antisocial behavior in preschool children changes from physical
to verbal forms with maturity. These behaviors may result from
frustration. Witnessing heated interchanges, either live or on
television, can also stir aggression in children. Finally,
biology -- hormones, temperament, physical appearance,
muscularity -- has a role in aggression.

Friendships tend to be formed among preschool-age children who
match each other in sex, age, and activity levels; and
friendships evolve among peers who talk, agree and share, offer
sympathy and help, and confide in each other. Children's
conceptions of friendship may change in stages. Selman suggests
that preschoolers first view friendships as momentary
playmateship, and then as one-way assistance.

Social understanding involves interpretation of others' emotions
and intentions, and appropriate responding to others'
expressions. The ability to interpret facial expressions is one
skill that develops in early childhood. However, preschoolers
have difficulty imagining mixed emotions or conflicting cues.

The formation of self-concept allows children to distinguish
themselves from others, and to know their social standing in the
family. An important aspect of self-concept is the child's sex.
Sex differences and gender roles highlights some of the many
studies that have tried to describe and explain differences
between boys and girls in the preschool period. Behavioral
differences between the sexes are observable in play behavior
(e.g., girls play house, boys play with trucks), nurturing

behaviors (e.g., girls become more nurturing than boys in this period), and aggressive behavior (e.g., boys tend to be more aggressive toward peers than girls). The bases of gender roles are probably some part biological, and some part learned. Gender roles are socially prescribed roles for males and females in a given culture. Parents, other adults, and even other children, contribute explicitly or implicitly to preschooler's developing self-concept and gender roles. Knowledge of sex and gender does not occur at the same rate. For example, 2- and 3-year-olds development of sex constancy occurs after they have a firm sense of gender identity. Young children's knowledge of gender roles is also too simplistic.

LEARNING OBJECTIVES

When you have finished studying Chapter 10 in both the text and this guide, you should be able to do the following:

1. Discuss how preschool children express their increasing autonomy, and what happens to children's attachment to parents as they become more autonomous.

2. Describe how parents' disciplinary styles differ and how these different styles affect children.

3. Suggest some ways other than direct commands and punishments that children learn appropriate social behaviors from their parents.

4. Describe stressors that modern families face and how these affect the family.

5. Discuss how siblings interact and learn from each other.

6. Characterize peer play for toddlers and preschoolers, and discuss the implications of peer play for social development.

7. Describe prosocial and antisocial behaviors and capacities among preschoolers.

8. List possible causes of anger and aggression among young children.

9. List the characteristics of friendships among preschool-age children.

10. Indicate the important factors that contribute to children's ability to understand and communicate with people in their social world.

11. Describe young children's self-concepts.

12. Compare young boys' and girls' social behaviors, play styles, and gender role development.

13. List the possible causes of sex differences in young children's social behaviors.

KEY TERMS

Terrible twos (p. 257)

Authoritarian parents (p. 258)

Permissive parents (p. 259)

Authoritative parents (p. 259)

Ritual play (p. 272)

Language play (p. 272)

Parallel play (p. 272)

Empathy (p. 273)

Prosocial (p. 273)

Self-concept (p. 278)

Gender roles (p. 282)

Sex constancy (p. 285)

Gender identity (p. 285)

STUDY QUESTIONS

1. Discuss the observable behavioral differences between 1-, 2-, 3-, and 4-year-old children who have been briefly separated from their mothers. (p. 256)

2. What are the major behavioral differences between securely and less securely attached children? (p. 258)

3. How do parent-child relationships change in the preschool years? Focus discussion on changes in parents' perceptions, expectations, and training patterns. (p. 258)

4. Discuss the parental disciplinary styles, and social and emotional consequences for children, described by Diana Baumrind. (pp. 258-261)

5. Explain how watching adults and instrumental conditioning affects children's social learning. (pp. 261-263)

6. Describe the common changes in family dynamics in the first two years following a divorce. (pp. 263-264)

7. How do boys and girls respond differently to divorce? (p. 264)

8. How does mother's work affect child care patterns? (pp. 264-268)

9.   Discuss the differences between children of working
     and non-working mothers. (pp. 264-268)

10. How do siblings interact and learn from each other?
     (pp. 268-279)

11. Describe the changes in children's play patterns in the
     preschool period. (pp. 271-272)

12. How do 2-year-olds differ from 7-year-olds in their
     prosocial skills? (pp. 273-274)

13. How do children learn to control anger and aggression?
     (p. 275)

14. What characteristics do preschoolers generally share with
     their playmates? (p. 276)

15. Describe the three stages of friendship identified by Robert
     Selman. (pp. 276-277)

16. How do boys and girls play styles, nurturing behaviors, and
     aggressive tendencies differ in the preschool period?
     (pp. 278-281)

17. How do parents' child-rearing attitudes and practices
     influence the development of gender roles? (pp. 282-284)

18. Discuss preschoolers' knowledge of sex constancy and gender
     identity. (pp. 284-287)

SELF-TEST, CHAPTER 10

COMPLETION

1. Researchers observe children separated from their parents to study the development of ~~attachment history~~

2. Although they venture farther away from their parents and tolerate longer separations from them, older children are no less _emotionally_ attached.

3. The phase of tantrums and acting-out among normal 2-year-olds is called the _terrible_ twos.

4. Like the children of authoritarian parents, children with permissive parents tend to be _dependent_ and unhappy, while children of authoritative parents tend to be _indepen_ , happy, and socially responsible.

5. _Compliments_ , or verbal praises, are more likely to reinforce behavior than tangible rewards, such as candy and toys.

6. At the present divorce rate, _half_ of the children born in this decade will live at least temporarily with one parent.

7. Children interact more _positively_ with parents than with siblings.

8. Sibling relationships are _reciprocal_ -- full of mutual imitation, play, and comforting, and fighting -- and complementary.

9. _Parallel Play_ play refers to play among 3- and 4-year-olds that is characterized by repetitive, rhythmic exchanges or turns, with exaggerated intonations, distorted rhythms, and broad gestures.

10. Older preschoolers are more likely than younger preschoolers to engage in _language_ play.

11. In _Parallel_ play, children play with toys that are like those of a nearby children but they do not actually play together.

12. _Empathy_ is a vicarious emotional response in which the emotions of the observer are similar to those of the person being observed.

EARLY CHILDHOOD

13. Between the ages of _2_ and 4, children become first more and then less aggressive.

14. There is a positive relation between blood levels of _testosterone_ and males' aggressive and antisocial behavior.

15. By the time they are 3, children can recognize and label _facial_ expressions that signal happiness, sadness, anger, and fear.

16. Preschoolers' self-concept is defined in terms of physical actions and possessions rather than _psychological_ attributes.

17. _gender_ roles are the ways of behaving that are socially prescribed for males and females in a particular culture.

18. The development of sex constancy requires experience and a degree of cognitive maturity not achieved by most children until age _6_ or even older.

19. By the age of _2_ or _3_ children have some sense of gender identity.

MULTIPLE CHOICE

1. Which of the following is characteristic of parents' responses to children's increasing autonomy?

    a. encourage child to be independent
    b. decreased physical contact with child
    c. relax constant attention and surveillance
    d. start fewer interactions
    e. all of the above

2. Children heavily disciplined in their first two or three years are likely to be:

    a. conforming
    b. hostile
    c. dependent
    d. aggressive
    e. a and c only

3. Research on divorce has shown which of the following to be TRUE?

    a. girls are more unruly than boys
    b. the divorce rate has declined since 1950
    c. mothers become more authoritarian and less affectionate
    d. fathers spend more time with their sons
    e. children blame their parents for the divorce

4. Which of the following statements about working mothers is FALSE?

   a. working mothers spend less time taking care of their children than do mothers who are housewives
   b. there is no difference in the amount of time working mothers and housewives spend alone with their children
   c. daughters of working mothers are more socially mature
   d. sons of working mothers tend to be less well adjusted socially and to achieve less in school
   e. single mothers who work tend to work less hours than married mothers who work

5. Circle the 3 stages of peer contact Mueller and Lucas observed among male toddlers.

   a. children watched each other but did not interact
   b. children saw friendships as fleeting things
   c. social bids were responded to and interactions increased
   d. boys tried to elicit not imitation but the appropriate complementary response
   e. friends were valued for their possessions

6. Which of the following prosocial actions is NOT likely to be done by a 2-year-old?

   a. comfort a crying person with hugs
   b. referee fights
   c. offer a distressed person something that is personally comforting to themselves
   d. offer suggestions
   e. b and d only

7. Which factor contributes to aggressiveness in young children

   a. frustration
   b. temperament
   c. physical appearance
   d. muscularity
   e. all of the above

8. Which of the following statements about sex differences and gender roles in preschoolers is FALSE?

   a. girls fantasies often are tied to everyday, domestic realities, while boys fantasies often are supernatural
   b. 3- and 4-year-old boys will not pay attention to a baby
   c. by the end of the preschool years girls are more nurturing than boys
   d. in all cultures, boys act more aggressive than girlse. boys engage in more rough-and-tumble play than girls do
   e. none of the above

9.   Which of the following statements about parents'
      child-rearing attitudes and practices is TRUE?

      a. boys are generally given more room to explore than girls
      b. when they read a story together, parents are more likely
          to interrupt sons than daughters
      c. girls are treated like boys until about the age of 3
      d. fathers are more authoritarian with their daughters
      e. fathers encourage expressiveness with their sons

MATCHING

Mark the letter of the matching answer in the space provided
beside each statement related to social and emotional
development.

        e   1. permissive parents
        b   2. family stressors
        f   3. one-way assistance
        a   4. authoritarian parents
        g   5. authoritative parents
        d   6. language play
        c   7. daughters of working mothers

a. firm, punitive unsympathetic, detached parents
b. divorce and full-time jobs for both parents
c. have a female model of social competence and high status
d. rhyming, saying nonsense words, and playing with words
e. do not exert control over their children
f. children take into account only their own needs and
    satisfaction in friendships
g. parents who see rights and responsibilities of parents and
    children as complementary
h. tend to be less well adjusted socially
i. use instrumental conditioning to train children
j. securely attached

ANSWERS TO THE SELF-TEST, CHAPTER 10

COMPLETION QUESTIONS

1. autonomy (p. 256)
2. emotionally (p. 257)
3. terrible (p. 257)
4. dependent, independent (pp. 261-262)
5. compliments (pp. 261-262)
6. half (p. 263)
7. positively (p. 269)
8. reciprocal (p. 270)
9. ritual (p. 272)
10. language (p. 272)
11. parallel (p. 272)
12. empathy (p. 273)
13. 2 (p. 274)
14. testosterone (p. 276)
15. facial (p. 277)
16. psychological (p. 278)
17. gender (p. 282)
18. 6 (p. 285)
19. 2, 3 (p. 285)

MULTIPLE CHOICE

1. e (p. 257)
2. e (p. 260)
3. c (pp. 263-264)
4. e (pp. 264-268)
5. a, c, d (p. 271)
6. e (pp. 273-274)
7. e (pp. 274-276)
8. b (pp. 278-281)
9. a (pp. 282-284)

MATCHING

1. e (p. 259)
2. b (p. 263)
3. f (p. 276)
4. a (p. 258)
5. g (p. 259)
6. d (p. 272)
7. c (p. 266)

CHAPTER SUMMARY

Chapter 11 outlines <u>physical development</u> in the middle childhood
years, roughly ages 6 to the onset of puberty. Physical growth
and skills during this period are briefly described, handicaps
some children cope with are discussed, and behavioral disorders
such as hyperactivity, autism, and learning disabilities are
examined.

<u>Physical growth and skills</u> charts changes in children's bodies
and behavior in the 5-7 years before puberty. Growth slows down
during this time, and children become more coordinated. Girls
are taller than boys from 7-10 years, but by age 10 the trend is
reversed and continues into adulthood. Differences in the
physical shape and abilities of boys and girls are slight during
the middle childhood years. Physical activity in children this
age has many benefits, including raising self-esteem as children
master skills, increasing how competently they are viewed by
peers, preventing risk factors for cardiovascular disease from
developing, and improving performance at school.

Physical <u>handicaps</u> affect 10-20 percent of school children at any
given time. If sensory impairment, mental retardation, and
behavior disorders are included, then a third or more children
suffer from one or more chronic disorders. Chronic disorders
include asthma, heart problems, cerebral palsy, orthopedic
problems, and diabetes. Vision problems are common, afflicting
one-fourth of all elementary school children. Ten to 20 percent
have reading problems. Other impairments are more rare, ranging
from 1-3 percent. Risk factors for cardiovascular disease,
cancer, and stroke include overweight, high blood pressure, high
blood cholesterol, poor physical fitness and diabetes, and are
common in children. Efforts are being made to educate youngsters
about these risks and to prevent them from developing.

<u>Behavior disorders</u> discussed in this section include
hyperactivity, autism, and learning disabilities. <u>Hyperactivity</u>,
almost exclusively seen in boys, is the most common behavior
disorder child psychiatrists treat. Treatments include
psychotherapy, psychoactive drugs such as Ritalin, and special
education. Hyperactive children are restless, distractible,
impulsive, easily angered and frustrated, aggressive and
destructive. Although different situations affect these children
in different ways, almost all hyperactive kids have problems in
school. Many of these problems stem from an inability to focus
attention and control impulses. These children also have
problems relating to peers. Genetic factors contribute to the
development of hyperactivity, and it is now thought there is a
physiological basis to the disorder. Environmental factors that
may contribute to this disorder include diet (sugar, additives,
food allergies), exposure to radiation, maternal alcohol

consumption during pregnancy, stress, chronic low lead levels, and fluorescent lighting. Autism, a form of psychosis, is a rare but devastating childhood disorder generally affecting children before the age of two-and-a-half. Characterized by an inability to communicate or to form social relationships, the causes of autism have not been clearly identified. Possible causal factors include biochemical imbalances (serotonin, zinc), brain damage, and genetic abnormality. Early damage to the left hemisphere is common in autistic children; the right hemisphere is often unaffected. Learning disabilities may include problems with reading or spelling (dyslexia), with arithmetic (dyscalcula), or with writing (dysgraphia). Learning disabled children lag behind several grades in reading and spelling. Dyslexics process visual information slowly, and can remember sounds but not images of words. While reading, letters may overlap in their visual field (masking), making the task difficult. Perseveration, poor visual memory, and memory fatigue are also problems. Most learning disabilities are inherited.

LEARNING OBJECTIVES

When you have finished studying Chapter 11 in both the text and this guide, you should be able to do the following:

1. Describe physical changes occurring in the middle childhood years.

2. Cite positive effects of physical activity in childhood.

3. Note the types and frequency of physical handicaps during this period.

4. List the risk factors for cardiovascular disease, cancer, and stroke that begin to develop in childhood.

5. Define hyperactivity and discuss it's causes, consequences, and treatments.

6. Describe autism, it's causes and treatments.

7. Differentiate between the types of learning disabilities, and explain the processing problems associated with dyslexia.

8. Cite the causes of learning disabilities.

KEY TERMS

Hyperactivity (p. 294)

Attention deficit disorder (p. 295)

Ritalin (p. 296)

Type A (p. 297)

Type B (p. 297)

Autism (p. 298)

Learning disabilities (p. 298)

Dyscalcula (p. 298)

Dysgraphia (p. 298)

Dyslexia (p. 298)

Masking (p. 299)

STUDY QUESTIONS

1. Discuss how physical development in middle childhood differs from development several years earlier. Describe any sex differences apparent at this age. (p. 292)

2.   What are some advantages associated with being physically
     active at this age? (p. 292)

3.   Describe the prevalence of risk factors for the major
     "lifestyle" diseases -- cardiovascular disease, stroke,
     and cancer -- that first develop in childhood.
     What is being done to alter these factors? (pp. 292-293)

4.   What are the common physical handicaps faced by elementary
     school children? (pp. 293-294)

5.   Describe what a typical hyperactive child might be like --
     physically, socially, emotionally, intellectually.
     (pp. 294-297)

6.   What theories have been advanced to explain hyperactivity?
     How strong is the evidence for these theories? (pp. 295-296)

7. How is hyperactivity typically treated? What are some
    advantages and disadvantages to these treatments?
    (pp. 296-297)

8. What is autism and what is thought to cause it? (p. 298)

9. Dyslexia is one type of learning disability. Explain the
    processing problems dyslexics have and how this impacts
    their school performance. (pp. 298-300)

10. Describe recent work on the Type A behavior pattern in
    children. (pp. 296-297)

MIDDLE CHILDHOOD

SELF-TEST, CHAPTER 11

COMPLETION QUESTIONS

1. In middle childhood boys and girls grow an average of _____ inches and gain about _____ pounds annually.

2. About _____ percent of elementary school children have vision problems.

3. _____ is a common psychoactive drug used to treat hyperactivity.

4. _____ and _____ therapies are effective in helping hyperactive children improve their social behavior and manage their anger.

5. _____ is one neurotransmitter investigated for a potential role in autism.

6. A learning problem in reading or spelling is termed _____, in arithmetic _____, and in writing _____.

7. _____ occurs when the contours of letters are similar and overlap in the visual field of a dyslexic.

8. Although some learning disabilities result from brain injuries, most are _____.

9. _____ handicaps may be just as disabling as physical handicaps.

10. Type A behavior in children is important for its potential relationship to _____ disease.

MULTIPLE CHOICE

1. Which of the following statements about physical development in middle childhood is TRUE?

    a. boys are taller than girls after about age 8
    b. girls have more flexible bodies than boys
    c. girls are more coordinated than boys
    d. children gain about 10 pounds per year
    e. children grow an average of 5 inches annually

2. Physical activity in middle childhood has been shown to have all but which of the following effects?

   a. increases self-esteem
   b. increases ratings of competence by peers
   c. prevent the development of cardiovascular risk factors
   d. improve sibling relationships
   e. increase school performance

3. Including sensory impairment, mental retardation, and behavior disorders, _____ percent of elementary school children suffer from one or more chronic disorders.

   a. 10 to 20
   b. 20 to 30
   c. 30 to 40
   d. 40 to 50
   e. 50 to 60

4. Behavioral interventions can affect all but which of the following cardiovascular risk factors?

   a. overweight
   b. high blood pressure
   c. high blood cholesterol
   d. poor physical fitness
   e. family history

5. All but which of the following terms describes the typical hyperactive child?

   a. male
   b. impulsive
   c. unpredictable
   d. aggressive
   e. focused

6. Which of the following has not been advanced as a theory to explain hyperactivity?

   a. dietary factors
   b. heavy maternal drinking during pregnancy
   c. stress
   d. chronic low lead levels
   e. iridescent lighting

7. Ritalin

     a. may interfere with a child's sleep patterns
     b. calms hyperactive children
     c. may affect growth patterns
     d. is a stimulant
     e. a, b, and c

8. Autism

     a. is a form of neurosis
     b. affects 4 or 5 of every 1,000 children
     c. is accompanied by mental retardation about one-fourth of
        the time
     d. typically affects the left hemisphere functions of the
        brain
     e. probably does not have a genetic component

9. Dyslexic children have normal

     a. hearing ability
     b. reading ability
     c. memory retention skills
     d. visual processing capabilities
     e. spelling ability

10. Most learning disabilities

     a. result from brain injuries to the left hemisphere
     b. result from brain injuries to the right hemisphere
     c. are inherited
     d. can be cured using psychoactive drugs such as Ritalin
     e. a and d only

MATCHING

Using the letters below, indicate whether each description is
more true of boys, more true of girls, or equally true of both
boys and girls. If the text does not specify a sex difference,
assume none exists.

_____ 1. high blood pressure
_____ 2. dyslexic
_____ 3. stronger forearm
_____ 4. diabetic
_____ 5. learning disabled
_____ 6. flexible
_____ 7. attention deficit disorder
_____ 8. mental retardation
_____ 9. taller at age 8
_____ 10. taller at age 12

a. more true of boys
b. more true of girls
c. equally true of both boys and girls (or no difference
   stated in the text)

ANSWERS TO THE SELF-TEST, CHAPTER 11

COMPLETION QUESTIONS

1. 2 1/2, 5 (p. 292)
2. 25 (p. 293)
3. Ritalin (p. 296)
4. Cognitive; behavioral (p. 297)
5. Serotonin (p. 298)
6. dyslexia; dyscalcula; dysgraphia (p. 298)
7. Masking (p. 299)
8. inherited (p. 300)
9. psychological (p. 294)
10. heart (pp. 296-297)

MULTIPLE CHOICE

1. b (p. 292)
2. d (p. 292)
3. c (p. 293)
4. e (p. 293)
5. e (pp. 294-295)
6. e (pp. 295-296)
7. e (p. 296)
8. d (p. 298)
9. a (pp. 298-300)
10. c (p. 300)

MATCHING

1. c (p. 293)
2. c (p. 298)
3. a (p. 292)
4. c (p. 293)
5. c (p. 298)
6. b (p. 292)
7. c (p. 295)
8. c (p. 293)
9. b (p. 292)
10. a (p. 292)

CHAPTER SUMMARY

Chapter 12 describes the cognitive advances children make in the middle childhood years. Changes in the way children think and the way they reason about moral issues are discussed. Growth of memory and memory strategies are explained, and data on individual differences in intelligence are presented, including a discussion of sex differences. Finally, contextual impacts on cognitive development are addressed. These include teacher expectations, the structure of classrooms, and the use of computers in learning.

Concrete operational thought is a logical way of reasoning about objects. This type of thinking, according to Piaget, develops about age 7. Children can only reason about concrete, tangible things, but are able to perform mental manipulations (operations) on things in an organized, systematic way. They understand the notions of reversibility and reciprocity, and are able to focus on and coordinate more than one dimension at the same time (decentering). Being able to conserve, that is understanding that things remain the same quantity but can look different, is a hallmark of this stage. Conservation of number occurs first, followed by length, liquid quantity, mass, weight, and volume. Conservation abilities affect perceptions of humor.

Concrete thought is a central facet of moral reasoning in middle childhood also. At about age 7 children's moral reasoning is guided by an external morality. Rules are believed to be established by authority figures, and are seen as absolute and unchangeable. At about age 11 children reach a level of internal morality, and understand that rules may be altered. Motives are now considered in evaluating the "badness" of an act.
Transitions in moral reasoning occur by trying to resolve conflicts between reasoning at different levels. Although they don't fully understand it, children prefer moral reasoning at levels more advanced than their own. Exposure to such reasoning appears to hasten transitions between stages. Training in moral reasoning has several forms. Children may be (1) directly instructed on how to reason at higher levels, (2) exposed to adults who are reasoning at stages higher than theirs, (3) asked to discuss moral issues with other children, or (4) asked to reflect on moral dilemmas common to them, given higher-level solutions, and asked to try these out. There is no consensus on the best way to advance children's moral reasoning.

Memory in middle childhood is better than at younger ages, and continues to improve with age. One reason for this is that older children use deliberate strategies. These include rehearsal (repeating something until it is memorized), organization (grouping items into meaningful chunks), imagery (imagining

pictures of items), and elaboration (linking unrelated items).
Spontaneous rehearsal is rare among five year olds but common
among 10 year olds. Rehearsal can be trained, and does improve
recall. Organization of information improves memory capabilities.
Two year olds can remember related items better than unrelated
ones, and tend to categorize words by how they sound or by their
functions. School aged children categorize words by their
meaning, and organize more according to taxonomy. Memory is also
assisted by social and spatial information and by story lines.
Organizational strategies can be trained, but the effects are
weak for preschoolers. Organizational ability improves through
middle childhood. Imagery strengthens recall and can also be
trained. Imagery may work for a variety of reasons. Elaboration
is used more by older children, and works better for older
children when it is self-generated. Experimenter-generated
elaboration works better for younger children. Metamemory is
what people know of their own memory processes. Preschoolers
and school aged children know a few things about memory, but
this does not directly predict performance on a memory task.
School aged children have accumulated much more knowledge of
routines or scripts, of concepts, and of facts than
preschoolers, which increases their ability to remember things.
Knowledge of a subject simplifies and speeds up encoding, and
gives a child a greater ability to draw inferences and integrate
information. Basic processes describes how short-term memory
capacity increases with age; however, this is debated.

There are wide individual differences in cognition, including
intelligence. Intelligence testing began around the start of this
century. Most intelligence tests derive an intelligence quotient
(IQ) -- a ratio of mental abilities to chronological age. On IQ
tests today, the mean equals 100 and the standard deviation
equals 15. Two-thirds of all people have IQs between 85 and 115;
95% have IQs between 70 and 130. Changes have been made in IQ
tests over the years, including the addition of tests of abstract
thinking and use of verbal symbols. The Stanford-Binet test and
the Wechsler Intelligence Scale for Children (WISC-R) are the two
most popular intelligence tests, and both test a variety of
abilities. The fairness and usefulness of IQ tests has been
debated. Many IQ tests are biased toward knowledge reflecting
white, middle-class culture. Yet, they do predict school success
and economic success in adulthood. To avoid cultural biases, IQ
tests of spatial perception and reasoning such as the Raven
Progressive Matrices Test have been developed. Creativity, based
on divergent thinking, is not tapped by standard intelligence
tests. Motivation improves IQ scores, and scores on IQ tests
generally increase over time, but are not stable or useful for
predicting success until age 12. Several alternatives have been
proposed to evaluate intelligence. There are also sex
differences in cognition. Girls consistently demonstrate greater
verbal ability than boys. They learn to read sooner and by
middle childhood understand and use language more than boys. Boys

consistently show greater spatial ability than girls, and by age 12 do better on math problems. Evidence suggesting a biological basis for sex differences is not strong. Differential play by boys and girls, and parental and teacher expectations and attitudes contribute to observed sex differences.

Finally, environmental influences on children's cognitive development are discussed in the section The context of cognitive development. Teacher's expectations, influenced by many factors, affect children's academic self-concepts, which in turn influence work patterns and feelings about learning. Open classrooms, with fewer physical boundaries, appear to hinder children's learning. Less structured classrooms also negatively affect children's performance. Learning from computers charts the powerful ways children can learn from interactive contact with them. Computers are especially helpful in assisting children to write and to think logically and systematically.

LEARNING OBJECTIVES

When you have finished studying Chapter 12 in both the text and this guide, you should be able to do the following:

1. Describe how children's thinking in middle childhood is distinct from thought processes in early childhood.

2. Define conservation, list terms associated with it, and note in which order children learn to conserver properties.

3. Explain developments in moral reasoning occurring in middle childhood.

4. Explain what drives transitions between stages of moral development.

5. Describe approaches to training children to reason at higher moral levels.

6. Identify memory strategies, and note how the memory capabilities of children in middle and early childhood differ.

7. Define metamemory and explain how it affects children's memory.

8. Explain how differences in knowledge between younger and older children affects differences in memory.

9. Describe differences in memory processing capabilities of younger and older children.

10. Define IQ and describe the content of intelligence tests.

11. Discuss the controversy surrounding the fairness of IQ tests, and what efforts have been made to address this.

12. Describe stability and change in IQ scores.

13. List the documented cognitive differences between boys and girls, and describe the theories advanced to explain these differences.

14. Discuss the effects of environmental factors -- teacher's expectations, openness of classrooms, classroom structure, and computers -- on children's abilities and performance.

KEY TERMS

Concrete operational thought (p. 304)

Decenter (p. 304)

External morality (p. 306)

Internal morality (p. 311)

Preconventional moral reasoning (p. 307)

Conventional moral reasoning (p. 307)

Postconventional moral reasoning (p. 307)

Rehearsal (p. 313)

Metamemory (p. 315)

Short-term memory (p. 317)

Intelligence Quotient (IQ)(p. 318)

Standard deviation (p. 318)

Convergent thinking (p. 322)

Divergent thinking (p. 322)

Open classroom (p. 329)

Closed classroom (p. 329)

Structured class (p. 330)

STUDY QUESTIONS

1. Describe what it means for a child to display concrete operational thought. (pp. 304-305)

2. Give some examples of how a child's conservation abilities could affect non-laboratory tasks. (pp. 305-306)

MIDDLE CHILDHOOD

3.   Explain the changes in moral reasoning children display in
      middle childhood, and how these changes mirror advances in
      other types of reasoning. (pp. 306-311)

4.   How do children move to higher levels of moral reasoning?
      Cite various methods used to train children to reason at
      higher levels. (pp. 311-312)

5.   Children in middle childhood remember more and better than
      younger children, and memory continues to improve with age.

      (a) How do differences in memory strategies explain these
          age effects? (pp. 312-315)

      (b) How do differences in metamemory explain these age
          effects? (pp. 315-316)

      (c) How do differences in knowledge explain these age
          effects? (pp. 316-317)

(d) How do differences in memory processing explain these age effects? (pp. 317-318)

6. Describe the composition of intelligence tests, and note how tests have changed over the years. (pp. 318-319)

7. Discuss the debate surrounding the fairness and usefulness of intelligence tests. (pp. 319-322)

8. IQ scores are more stable and valid after age 12. What changes in cognitive processing would explain this fact? (pp. 322-324)

9. Describe the sex differences in cognition for which there is good evidence. (pp. 324-325)

MIDDLE CHILDHOOD

10. Cite the various theories attempting to explain the origins of sex differences. (pp. 325-327)

11. The environment exerts powerful impacts on children's cognitive development.

    (a) How do teachers influence children's academic self-concepts? (pp. 327-328)

    (b) How does the physical classroom set-up affect children's academic performance? (pp. 328-329)

    (c) How does the structure of the class affect children's academic performance? (pp. 329-330)

    (d) How do computers influence children's cognitive development? (pp. 330-332)

SELF-TEST, CHAPTER 12

COMPLETION QUESTIONS

1. Children who believe that rules are unable to be changed are operating according to an _external_ morality.

2. The recognition that one dimension may make up for another dimension is called _reciprocity_.

3. _Conflict_ resolution moves children from one stage of moral reasoning to another.

4. Grouping items into meaningful clusters or chunks is one memory strategy termed _organization_

5. _rehearsal_ is the process of repeating something until it is memorized.

6. Knowing that pairs of antonyms are easier to remember than unrelated words is an example of _metamemory_

7. Most people can only remember about __7__ separate chunks of information.

8. By age __12__ IQ test scores are stable and useful for predicting success.

9. The ratio of mental age to chronological age is called the _intelligence_ _quotient_.

10. Girls consistently have been found to have greater _verbal_ ability than boys, while boys have greater _spatial_ ability than girls.

11. Classrooms with few physical boundaries are called _open_ classrooms.

MULTIPLE CHOICE

1. The ability to focus and coordinate height and width at the same time is termed

   a. decentering
   b. reversibility
   c. reciprocity
   d. conservation
   e. an operation

2. Conservation of different quantities occurs in the following order :

   a. weight, liquid quantity, mass
   b. mass, number, length
   c. number, mass, volume
   d. volume, mass, weight
   e. length, number, mass

3. Piaget developed his theory of moral reasoning by watching and questioning children as they

   a. responded to a dilemma about Heinz and his wife
   b. played marbles
   c. invented stories
   d. argued with each other
   e. played with sex-typed toys

4. The funniest jokes

   a. pose a small challenge to a person's cognitive abilities
   b. are understandable
   c. are surprising
   d. b and c
   e. a, b, and c

5. Carol insists that God made the rules to her game of jacks, and the rules cannot be changed. Carol is operating according to an _____ morality, and is most likely _____ years old.

   a. external; 7
   b. external; 12
   c. internal; 7
   d. internal; 12
   e. none of the above

6. Which of the following strategies has not been employed as a means of increasing children's level of moral reasoning?

   a. exposing children to adults who are reasoning about dilemmas at varied levels
   b. having children discuss moral issues with other children
   c. having children discuss moral dilemmas that routinely occur in their lives
   d. directly training children to reason at certain levels
   e. teaching families to reinforce their children's improved moral reasoning

7. The mnemonic "In fourteen hundred and ninety-two Columbus sailed the ocean blue" is an example of

   a. rehearsal
   b. organization
   c. imagery
   d. elaboration
   e. metamemory

8. Regarding the memory strategy of organization, which of the following is NOT TRUE?

   a. related items are remembered better than unrelated items
   b. school age children are more likely than preschoolers to organize words by their meaning
   c. school age children are more likely than preschoolers to organize words by their function
   d. school age children are more likely than preschoolers to organize according to taxonomy
   e. children can be trained to use organizational strategies

9. Which of the following reasons has NOT been advanced to explain why imagery improves recall?

   a. imagery highlights associations between items to be remembered
   b. imagery provided two forms in which information may be recalled
   c. imagery makes learning pleasant, personal, and vivid
   d. imagery subjects the information to deeper levels of cognitive processing
   e. imagery is more easily learned than other strategies

10. Elaborations are more effective for middle school age children

    a. when they are active
    b. when they are experimenter-generated
    c. when they are self-generated
    d. a and b
    e. a and c

11. Training in which of the following does NOT improve memory retention?

    a. rehearsal
    b. organization
    c. imagery
    d. elaboration
    e. metamemory

12. Children in middle childhood remember more and better than younger children for all but which of the following reasons?

    a. older children receive more training from their parents on memory strategies
    b. older children know more sophisticated memorization and retrieval strategies
    c. older children are more flexible in tailoring strategies to situations
    d. older children know more about the subject matter
    e. older children have a larger, more efficient memory storage system

13. Approximately _____ percent of all people score between 85 and 115 on standard intelligence tests

    a. 33
    b. 50
    c. 67
    d. 95
    e. 99

14. The ability to code numbers into symbols, copy designs made with blocks, and put pictures into logical order are examples of

    a. items on the Stanford-Binet intelligence test
    b. items on the Iowa Test of Basic Skills
    c. items to test verbal intelligence
    d. items to test performance intelligence
    e. items to test divergent thinking

15. Standard intelligence tests

    a. are often culturally biased in favor of low income groups
    b. measure creativity well
    c. are nearly perfect measures of children's basic competence to think
    d. are highly predictive of school grades
    e. are not predictive of economic success in adulthood

16. Biological explanations for sex differences in cognition

    a. suggest that differences originate in the Y chromosome
    b. suggest that boys' brains may be less lateralized, and this accounts for differences in ability
    c. suggest that hormonal differences are responsible for differing abilities
    d. have received widespread empirical support
    e. all of the above

17. Which is NOT TRUE when teachers have high expectations of students

    a. teachers talk more
    b. teachers teach more challenging material
    c. teachers criticize more
    d. teachers pay closer attention
    e. teachers praise students more

18. Students in open, compared with closed, classrooms

    a. do better on tests of mathematical concepts
    b. complain about feeling crowded
    c. score higher on tests of creative thinking
    d. are exposed to less noise
    e. are less competitive

19. Structured classes

    a. appear to work best for children who need to know what is expected of them
    b. produce less academic progress than open classrooms
    c. produce more creative thinking than open classrooms
    d. allow children to work at their own pace
    e. none of the above

20. Children seem drawn to computers because

    a. they respond immediately
    b. they do not blame children for mistakes
    c. they do not play favorites
    d. they are objective
    e. all of the above

MATCHING

Match the phrase with the corresponding term or terms below.
More than one response may be correct.

___ 1. affects the development of spatial abilities
___ 2. may reinforce sex differences
___ 3. influence of teacher expectations on student performance
___ 4. possible reason for greater verbal ability in girls
___ 5. one effect of computers

a. early maturation   f. tests
b. improved composition skills   g. textbooks
c. improved logical reasoning   h. toy play
d. Pygmalion effect   i. Y chromosome

ANSWERS TO THE SELF-TEST, CHAPTER 12

COMPLETION QUESTIONS

1. external (p. 306)
2. reciprocity (p. 304)
3. conflict (p. 311)
4. organization (p. 315)
5. rehearsal (p. 313)
6. metamemory (p. 316)
7. 7 (p. 314)
8. 12 (p. 324)
9. intelligence quotient (p. 318)
10. verbal, spatial (p. 324)
11. open (p. 329)

MULTIPLE CHOICE

1. a (p. 304)
2. c (p. 305)
3. b (p. 306)
4. d (p. 305)
5. a (p. 306)
6. e (pp. 311-312)
7. d (p. 315)
8. c (pp. 314-315)
9. e (p. 315)
10. e (p. 315)
11. e (pp. 313-316)
12. a (p. 318)
13. c (p. 318)
14. d (p. 319)
15. d (pp. 319-321)
16. c (p. 326)
17. c (p. 328)
18. b (pp. 329-330)
19. a (p. 330)
20. e (p. 331)

MATCHING

1. h (p. 325)
2. e, f, and g (pp. 326-327)
3. d (p. 328)
4. a (p. 326)
5. b or c (pp. 331-332)

CHAPTER SUMMARY

Topics discussed in this chapter on Social and emotional
development in middle childhood include the importance of family
and peer relationships, growing social understanding, and the
development of a greater knowledge of the self.

Family relationships discusses the significant role families play
in middle childhood. Ideally, family rules at this age should
strike a balance between permissiveness and restrictiveness.
Providing limits without being too restrictive assists children
in becoming independent. The shift from complete parental
regulation of a child's activities to coregulation by both parent
and child also assists in developing independence. In addition
to rules, the emotional quality of parents' interaction with
their children is related to children's behavior. An
authoritative (versus permissive or authoritarian) disciplinary
style is related to desired behaviors in children.

The section A society of children discusses the transitions
children make from family and home to friends and school. Peer
groups increase in importance at this age. The desire to achieve
a shared goal and a child's sex are two factors contributing to
group cohesiveness. Sex segregation becomes more marked in
middle childhood, and is influenced by our cultural norms. Girls'
interactions are more intimate and intensive; Boys' peer
interactions are more physical, competitive, goal-oriented and
extensive. Popularity with peers is affected by physical
attractiveness, power, and social interaction skills. Popular
kids are friendly, not aggressive, know what to say at the right
time, make good suggestions, give praise, play constructively and
cooperatively, and adapt to group norms. Rejected children act
inappropriately, are hyperactive or aggressive, and have problems
managing conflict. Rejected children can be taught to change
their behavior to improve popularity. Friendship is important
because it offers opportunities to learn social skills like
communication, cooperation, and self-control. Friendships also
provide support in times of need, and lay the groundwork for
future relationships. Most children have at least one friend.
During middle childhood friendships develop from one-sided
affairs to cooperative, sympathetic, mutual exchanges -- two way
relationships. However, serious conflict can ruin friendships at
this age. By 11 or 12, sharing, trust, loyalty and support are
cited as important qualities in friendships.

Children engage in a variety of activities with age-mates.
Playing games and sports -- both formal and informal -- is common
and useful. In the past three decades, games have become less
formal, less rough, and more likely to include girls. Helping,
and sharing, cooperating and competing outlines changes in these
behaviors. Helping and showing concern in some situations may

decline toward the end of middle childhood, while competitiveness increases. Competitiveness, not always adaptive, is partially the result of the specific situation and our cultural values. Boys are especially rewarded for competing while girls are rewarded for cooperating. Generosity of both boys and girls increases during middle childhood, but is affected by personal and situational factors. Almost all children lie and cheat at some time. Circumstances affect honesty in nearly all children. Obedience is least likely if an adult model is observed performing the behavior and doesn't get caught. Moral behavior may be fostered by (1) punishing wrongdoing immediately, (2) attributing moral qualities to children, or (3) explaining why a child should act in certain ways and stressing the effects of the child's behaviors. Freud believed identification with a parent and the development of guilt feelings was central to the development of morality. However, research suggests identification with other adults is just as effective in producing a conscience. Acting aggressively without an instrumental purpose begins to occur in middle childhood, and increases steadily with age. Rejecting, unloving parents who are in conflict with each other, who punish their children for aggression by do not reward them for cooperation or sharing, produce aggressive kids. Children learn to be aggressive from family members and peers, and from the structure and activities of play groups. Children's perceptions and cognitions and television also contribute to aggression.

Social understanding of others and social rules increases during the school years. Children's understanding of other peopleincreases with age as they learn to infer more about people's internal states and thoughts. About age 10 children begin to incorporate psychological attributes in their descriptions of others. Children learn a lot about social rules and understand social conventions by school age. A children grow older, appreciation for the distinctions between social conventions and other rules, for flexibility of rules, and for subtle social rules develops. Children become more adept at solving social problems as they age. This ability is preceded by cognitive understanding.

The final section, The self, discusses how children's views of themselves change during this time. Children's identity -- their views of themselves -- changes dramatically. Descriptions of self are very concrete initially, but contain more psychological attributes toward the end of middle childhood. About age 8, children begin to understand the difference between self and body. Self-esteem -- a reflection of mastery of developmental tasks, performance on schoolwork, and success in solving social problems, as well as others' reactions to them -- deepens during this time. Middle childhood is a critical period in the development of self-esteem because complex evaluations are made, and these are difficult to change. Low self-esteem may have psychological consequences. High self-esteem is associated with independence, creativity, peer social acceptance, assertiveness, and warm, supportive, attentive, authoritative parents. Studies of the continuity of personality suggest that a few temperamental traits such as activity level, intensity, adaptability, and rhythmicity are stable from infancy to early adulthood. Aggressiveness and sociability appear stable during childhood and beyond.

LEARNING OBJECTIVES

When you have finished studying Chapter 13 in both the text and this guide, you should be able to do the following:

1. Discuss how children's relationships with peers change between early and middle childhood.

2. Describe the ideal relationship between rules and freedom during middle childhood. Why is this important?

3. Describe what it means to be an authoritative parent, and how this affects children.

4. Cite factors contributing to the development of peer relationships.

5. Note how peer relationships of boys and girls differ.

6. List the attributes of popular versus rejected children. Note what can be done to assist rejected children.

7. Explain why friendships are important to children at this age, and how they change between the ages of 7 and 12.

8. Describe the role games and sports play in middle childhood.

9. Chart changes in helping, sharing, cooperation, and competition during middle childhood.

10. Describe circumstances in which children would be likely to cheat or disobey instructions, and how this might be prevented.

11. Explain Freud's views of moral behavior and the research which supports or refutes his theory.

12. Describe contributions to the development of aggression in children.

13. Note how children's understanding of social rules and of people changes during the school years.

14. Explain changes in how children view themselves during middle childhood.

15. Discuss contributions to self-esteem, correlates of high and low self-esteem and explain why middle childhood is a critical period for the development of self-esteem.

16. Note which personality traits appear stable.

KEY TERMS

Intensive peer relations (p. 339)

Extensive peer relations (p. 339)

Social conventions (p. 352)

Identity (p. 357)

Self-esteem (p. 357)

STUDY QUESTIONS

1. How do rules influence children's behavior in middle childhood? (pp. 336-337)

2. Describe the impact of parenting styles on children's behavior. (p. 337)

3. Explain how peer groups are formed and how girls' and boys' peer groups differ. (pp. 337-339)

4. Describe the factors affecting judgments of popularity. Do these differ appreciably from those seen in adulthood? Describe a popular and unpopular child. (pp. 339-340)

5. Discuss the functions of friendship for a school age child. (pp. 341-342)

6. Note the role of sports and games in childhood. (pp. 342-343)

7. How and why does prosocial behavior change in middle childhood? (pp. 343-346)

8.   What factors influence the development of competitiveness in children at this age? (pp. 343-346)

9.   How is dishonesty affected by circumstance? (pp. 346-348)

10.   Describe factors associated with increased moral behavior, including Freud's views on the topic. (pp. 346-348)

11.   How is aggressive behavior fostered? (pp. 348-350)

12.   What changes in middle childhood facilitate greater social understanding? (pp. 350-356)

13. Define self-esteem and discuss why middle childhood is such a critical period for self-esteem development. (pp. 356-358)

14. Aggressiveness appears to be a stable trait during childhood and beyond. What are some implications of this stability? (pp. 360-362)

15. Describe some unique features of the Thomas and Chess research presented in the text. (pp. 358-360)

16. The research presented in the lifespan focus section had some interesting findings related to the stability of personality. What were they? (p. 361)

SELF-TEST, CHAPTER 13

COMPLETION QUESTIONS

1. In contrast to boys, who have _extensive_ peer relations, girls have _intensive_ peer relations.

2. In talking about their friends, _girls_ are likely to dwell on how their friends look and on their personalities.

3. Rejected children may have trouble managing _conflict or anger_

4. In Freud's view of moral development, a child must identify with the parent in order for the _conscience_ to be formed.

5. According to Freud, moral sanctions emanate from within once the child has developed a sense of _guilt_.

6. Beginning at about age _seven_, the effects of television seem to intensify.

7. Over the school years, children learn to infer more about people's _internal_ states and thoughts.

8. By age _6_, children understand that inner thoughts and outward expressions may be inconsistent.

9. _Social conventions_ are culturally defined and arbitrary rules establishing dress codes, forms of address, and table manners.

10. The _authoritative_ parenting style is associated with high self-esteem in children.

MULTIPLE CHOICE

1. In a large survey of school age children, most said

   a. they liked their families
   b. they worried about their future
   c. their families imposed rules
   d. a and c only
   e. all of the above

2. Parents with an authoritative disciplinary style

   a. are warm and loving, but don't set limits
   b. are warm and loving, and do set limits
   c. let their children make their own rules
   d. have very strict rules
   e. produce withdrawn or hostile children

3. Research has indicated that _____ fosters peer group
   development and affects peer group cohesion.

   a. competition within the peer group
   b. competition with outside groups
   c. desire to achieve a shared goal
   d. a and c
   e. b and c

4. Sex segregation in middle childhood

   a. is less marked than in preschool
   b. is influenced by cultural norms
   c. is always more dominant than other factors such as age
   d. is stronger among girls than boys
   e. none of the above

5. In contrast to boys, girls

   a. form larger peer groups
   b. express fewer of their feelings to peers
   c. are less physical in their games with peers
   d. are more competitive in their interactions with peers
   e. play in larger physical spaces with peers

6. Attractive children are perceived by other children as

   a. wealthier
   b. taller
   c. more likely to be first born
   d. smarter
   e. favored by teachers

7. Which of the following is NOT associated with more
   popularity among peers

   a. attractiveness
   b. leadership
   c. being the top student
   d. knowing what to say
   e. friendliness

MIDDLE CHILDHOOD

8. Studies designed to change the behavior of unpopular children indicate that

    a. popularity ratings increase after training, but the increase is temporary
    b. popularity ratings increase after training and remain elevated for at least a year
    c. popularity ratings only increase if the parents and siblings of the unpopular child are involved
    d. nearly all unpopular children are aware of the effects of their behavior on others
    e. there is little researchers can do to change children's behavior and thus affect their popularity status

9. Which of the following statements about friendships in middle childhood is NOT TRUE?

    a. friendships offer opportunities to learn social skills like communication and cooperation
    b. friendships change from one-sided relationships to cooperative, mutual exchanges
    c. friendships are not seriously affected by conflict
    d. friendships last longer as children grow older
    e. all of the above are true

10. Over the last 60 years, children's games

    a. have become more formal
    b. have become more rough
    c. have become more team-oriented
    d. have involved more equipment
    e. have involved more girls in active sports

11. Helping and showing concern in some situations

    a. declines in middle childhood
    b. increases in middle childhood
    c. increases for boys, but remains stable for girls
    d. increases for boys, but declines for girls
    e. increases for girls, but remains stable for boys

12. Which of the following does NOT increase in middle childhood?

    a. generosity
    b. competitiveness
    c. peer interaction
    d. aggressiveness
    e. prosocial behaviors

13. Moral behavior may be assisted by

   a. physically punishing children for misbehaving
   b. taking away toys or privileges
   c. showing children how their behavior affects others
   d. attributing moral qualities to them
   e. c and d

14. Which of the following statements is NOT TRUE? Children are most likely to act aggressively if they

   a. watch a lot of violent TV
   b. believe that TV shows are real and identify strongly with the aggressive characters
   c. have parents, especially fathers, who act aggressively toward them
   d. observe the aggression of their parents, friends, and heroes
   e. are the objects of aggression

15. In describing their classmates, as children age they move from _____ to _____ to _____ descriptions.

   a. physical, behavioral, psychological
   b. behavioral, physical, psychological
   c. physical, psychological, behavioral
   d. behavioral, psychological, physical
   e. psychological, behavioral, physical

MATCHING

Match the following characteristics with the appropriate term.

_____ 1. a prerequisite for solving social problems
_____ 2. a requirement for politeness
_____ 3. a correlate of high self-esteem
_____ 4. a stable trait across childhood and beyond
_____ 5. stable from infancy into early childhood

a. aggressiveness
b. activity level
c. competitiveness
d. formal operational thinking
e. generosity

f. having strict parents
g. independence
h. linguistic skills
i. perspective taking

ANSWERS TO THE SELF-TEST, CHAPTER 13

COMPLETION QUESTIONS

1. extensive, intensive (p. 339)
2. girls (p. 342)
3. conflict or anger (p. 340)
4. conscience (p. 347)
5. guilt (p. 347)
6. 8 or 9 (p. 350)
7. internal (p. 351)
8. 8 (p. 351)
9. social conventions (p. 352)
10. authoritative (p. 358)

MULTIPLE CHOICE

1. e (p. 336)
2. b (p. 337)
3. e (pp. 337-338)
4. b (pp. 338-339)
5. c (pp. 338-339)
6. d (p. 339)
7. c (pp. 339-340)
8. b (p. 340)
9. c (pp. 341-342)
10. e (p. 343)
11. a (p. 343)
12. e (pp. 341-348)
13. e (pp. 346-348)
14. c (p. 350)
15. a (p. 352)
16. c (p. 357)

MATCHING

1. i (p. 355)
2. h (p. 354)
3. g (p. 357)
4. a (p. 360)
5. b (p. 358)

CHAPTER SUMMARY

Chapter 14 begins the section on Adolescence by discussing
physical development of young people in adolescence, the ages
from 10 to 19 years. The section Puberty describes patterns of
growth, development of sexual characteristics, and the trend
toward earlier maturity. Puberty starts at the end of childhood
in the period of adolescence. This period is marked by radical
physical and psychological changes for the young person.
Biological changes, particularly in levels of hormones secreted
into the bloodstream, mark the onset of puberty. Hormones and
glands are predominantly responsible for influencing the
development of girls and boys into sexually mature young adults.
Puberty triggers a rapid growth spurt in height, muscles,
internal organs, and bones. The male growth spurt usually starts
at 12, peaks at 14, and stops by 19 years. Females usually begin
their growth spurt at 10, peak at 13, and stop at 18. Growth in
height results from the final stages of bone maturation and
varies widely from individual to individual, as does the growth
of organs and muscles. Growth in this period, infancy and early
childhood, is asynchronous. However, while growth in infancy and
early childhood was proximodistal (i.e., from center to
periphery), growth in puberty if distoproximal (i.e., from
periphery to center).

Development of sexual characteristics is a major earmark of
puberty, and enables the adolescent to reproduce. The
reproductive systems enlarge for both sexes, and become
functional. Both primary (e.g., genitals) and secondary (e.g.,
pubic hair) sexual characteristics develop at puberty. By the
end of puberty, boys are generally stronger than girls, while
girls are generally more flexible. Cultural attitudes magnify
these biological differences, and color girls' expectations for
and experience of their menstrual cycles. Statistics gathered
from industrialized countries indicate a trend toward earlier
maturity. Adolescents experience their growth spurt at an
earlier age, and grow taller and heavier than they did in the
past.

The section Effects of physical change discusses the complex
psychological changes associated with physical changes. The
extent of changes and timing of puberty have strong influences on
adolescents' behavior and self-image. Hormones and psychological
states points out links between hormones, emotions, and
behaviors. The exact nature of relations among these factors is
difficult to ascertain, since social, cultural, and psychological
factors may influence the affect of hormones on psychological
change. Physical changes accompanying puberty affect
adolescents' images of themselves. Many young adults are
dissatisfied with their appearance, or body image. Adolescents
with a favorable body image tend to be better adjusted, socially

ADOLESCENCE

and emotionally.

Feelings of mature sexuality also follow from the physical changes of puberty. Mature sexuality extends beyond physical maturity, and into the domain of awareness and participation in what is sexually appropriate behavior. This section discusses the influence of cultural expectations on sexual behavior during adolescence. In the past few decades, many attitudes and behaviors related to sexuality have changed for adolescents. Adolescents do not feel society disapproves of sexual activity, and manifest less guilt and more sexual activity. Many adolescents are sexually attracted to members of the same sex, and some even act on these feelings. Homosexual experiences that may occur in adolescence tend to occur earlier for girls than for boys. The causes of a person's homosexuality seem to be tangled in a complex biological, psychological and social web.

The section Health problems outlines common threats to the health and well-being of adolescents. Many of the problems result from a combination of physical and behavioral changes occurring in puberty. Pregnancy, childbirth, and contraception are topics that few adolescents have enough information about to make responsible decisions about sex. This probably results from cultural and parental attitudes about sex education. When sexual activity is mixed with ignorance of or lack of access to effective contraceptives, the sexually mature adolescent is likely to get pregnant. Teenage pregnancy is becoming increasingly common in the United States; and presents a serious problem to the adolescent who is physically, emotionally, or financially unable to meet the needs of an infant. Alcohol, drugs, and smoking are also common risk factors for adolescent health. Drug use is very common among high school students, especially drinking of alcohol. Drug use has physical (e.g., central nervous system damage), social (e.g., dangerous behavior) and psychological (e.g., memory and attention problems) consequences. Substance use and abuse is dependent on personality factors, peers, and family influences. Eating disorders, such as bulimia and anorexia nervosa, exist among adolescents. Adolescent girls are more susceptible to these problems, as they strive to meet a cultural ideal of thinness.

The chapter's concluding statement is that physical maturity and fitness is a positive experience for the majority of adolescents.

LEARNING OBJECTIVES

When you have finished studying Chapter 14 in both the text and this guide, you should be able to do the following:

1. Discuss the biological changes experienced by adolescents during puberty.

2. Describe growth changes during adolescents' growth spurt.

3. Describe the development of sexual characteristics in male and female adolescents.

4. Discuss the possible reasons for the trend toward earlier maturity over the past century.

5. Discuss the hypothesized links between hormonal activity and psychological states.

6. Define body image and discuss the common concerns of adolescents concerning their body image.

7. Describe how adolescent sexual behaviors and how cultural expectations regarding those behaviors have changed in the last 50 years.

8. Discuss the homosexual feelings and experiences in adolescence, noting the differences between male and female experiences.

9. Discuss the personal and social problems associated with teenage pregnancy.

10. Discuss the effects and possible predictors of alcohol and drug use among adolescents.

11. Describe the nature of and potential causes of eating disorders such as bulimia and anorexia nervosa.

KEY TERMS

Adolescence (p. 368)

Puberty (p. 368)

Growth spurt (p. 369)

Secondary sexual characteristics (p. 370)

ADOLESCENCE

Menarche (p. 372)

Body image (p. 375)

Late maturers (p. 376)

Early maturers (p. 376)

Sexual scripts (p. 378)

Bulimia (p. 386)

Anorexia nervosa (p. 386)

STUDY QUESTIONS

1. Discuss the biological changes occurring during puberty.
    Note in particular hormonal activity in this period.
    (pp. 368-369)

2. Describe the changes in body size, including height and
    organ growth, during the growth spurt. How do males and
    females differ in their growth spurts? (pp. 369-371)

3. Describe the differences in size, shape, and strength of
    males and females resulting from the development of
    secondary sexual characteristics and other physical
    changes during adolescence. (pp. 371-372)

4. How have growth trends changed in the past century, and
    what are the potential causes of these changing trends?
    (pp. 372-373)

5. How might changes in hormonal activity affect
    psychological states? (pp. 373-374)

6. What physical changes create concern in adolescents
    about their body image? (p. 375)

7. How have adolescent sexual habits changed in the last 30
    years? (pp. 375-379)

8.   What are sexual scripts, and how do they differ for males and females? (pp 378-379)

9.   How do experiences and feelings about homosexuality differ for males and females in early to late adolescence? (p. 379)

10.   How might biological, psychological, emotional, family and social factors influence the development and expression of homosexuality? (p. 379)

11.   What are some of the special problems faced by pregnant adolescents? (pp. 380-383)

12.   How does the rate of teenage pregnancy in the United States compare with similar countries? (pp. 381-383)

13. Discuss how social and parental beliefs about sex education may influence the rate of teenage pregnancy. (p. 381-383)

14. How do personality, peer, and family factors influence adolescent use of alcohol and drugs? (pp. 383-385)

15. What are the possible causes and the effects of bulimia and anorexia nervosa? (pp. 385-386)

ADOLESCENCE

SELF-TEST, CHAPTER 14

COMPLETION QUESTIONS

1. _puberty_ refers to the set of biological changes that mark the beginning of adolescence.

2. _puberty_ begins as increased levels of hormones enter the bloodstream, in response to signals from the hypothalamus region of the brain.

3. The rise in levels of growth hormone cause sudden increases in growth known as a _growth spurt_.

4. For boys, the growth spurt usually starts at _12_ or _13_ peaks at about 14 years, and stops at _18_ or _19_.

5. For girls, the growth spurt starts at _10_ or _11_, peaks at 12 or 13, and stops at _17_ or _18_.

6. Sexual maturity is apparent in adolescence by the development of _second_ sexual characteristics.

7. Low levels of the sex hormone _estradiol_ may be related to psychological adjustment problems in 9- to 14-year-old girls.

8. Boys with high _adrenal androgens_ are more likely to have behavior problems -- rebelliousness, talking back, fighting -- or feelings of sadness and confusion.

9. Adolescents with a poor body _image_ do not like the way they look.

10. In contrast to late maturers, _early_ maturers are self-confident, calm, and considered mature by both adults and other adolescents.

11. In a study of 19-year-olds, it was found that _80_ percent of the boys and _70_ percent of the girls were sexually active.

12. Typically, boys have their first homosexual experience with an older boy or a man at ages _11_ or _12_; while girls are likely to have their first homosexual experience between the ages of _6_ or _10_.

13. The medical risks for a pregnant teenager are _2_ times greater than those of women who are pregnant in their 20s.

14. Teenagers get their information about sex from three principal sources: their _parents_, their _peers_, and _books_.

15. By the end of tenth grade, _90_ percent of all adolescents have drunk alcohol.

16. In the last few years, the number of adolescents using marijuana, sedatives, and tranquilizers has decreased, but the number using _heroin_ and other opiates has increased.

17. Drugs can damage the central nervous system and a person's abilities to pay _attention_ and _remember_

18. Cigarettes, unlike marijuana, are both psychologically and _physical_ addictive.

19. The pattern of alternate starving, gorging, and purging is called _binging_.

20. The eating disorder called _anorexia ner___ can lead to symptoms of dehydration, erratic heart rhythms, and other life-threatening conditions.

MULTIPLE CHOICE

1. Which of the following does NOT have a strong affect on females during puberty?

   (a.) testosterone
   b. adrenal androgens
   c. progesterone
   d. estrogen
   e. pituitary mammotropic hormones

2. During the male growth spurt, which of the following does NOT occur?

   a. testes enlarge
   b. penis enlarges
   c. gain muscle mass, strength and stamina
   (d.) first menstruation
   e. voice deepens

ADOLESCENCE

3. Which of the following is NOT evidence of the trend toward
    earlier maturity?

    a. girls in the United States are menstruating earlier than
       they did a century ago
    b. boys in the United States start their growth spurt two
       years earlier than boys did at the turn of the century
    c. adolescents grow taller than they did in the past
    d. adolescents are thinner now than in the past as a result
       of better eating habits
    e. armor worn by medieval knights would fit a 10-year-old
       today

4. Hormones have been linked to which of the following
    psychological phenomena during adolescence?

    a. changes in adolescent girls' self-image, attitudes toward
       others, and perceptual abilities
    b. psychological adjustment problems in girls
    c. aggression in boys
    d. sadness and confusion in boys
    e. all of the above

5. High levels of androgen may _____ aggression; when
    researchers gave adolescents androgen, they became
    _____ aggressive.

    a. decrease, less
    b. increase, more
    c. decrease, more
    d. increase, non-
    e. none of the above

6. A female adolescent's interpretation of her menstruation
    is NOT influenced by:

    a. her knowledge
    b. her expectations
    c. her levels of androgen
    d. her personality
    e. support from her family

7. When adolescents in the Berkeley Growth Study were
    observed at the age of 33, the late maturers exhibited
    which of the following characteristics?

    a. professional success
    b. rigid and tightly controlled behaviors
    c. impulsive, irritable, and rebellious
    d. flexibility, perceptiveness, and assertiveness
    e. c and d only

8. In a survey of 600 adolescents which of the following was NOT found?

   a. sex was ranked higher in importance than doing well in school
   b. sex was ranked lower in importance than having friends of the same sex
   c. participating in sports was ranked as more important than sex
   d. being romantically involved was ranked as more important than sex
   e. sexual activity was ranked as less important than doing well in school

9. Which of the following statements is NOT supported by research?

   a. all adolescents are sexually attracted to people of the other sex
   b. some adolescents wish for sexual relationships with members of their own sex
   c. boys who have had homosexual experiences typically have their first homosexual experience with boys much younger than themselves
   d. girls are most likely to have their first homosexual experience at a younger age than boys who have homosexual experiences
   e. c and d only

10. Adolescents in the United States are poor users of contraception because:

   a. young adolescents are too cognitively immature to understand the complexities that make up sexual reproduction
   b. many adolescents are not well educated on the facts of life
   c. adults believe that educating adolescents about sex and contraception will increase sexual promiscuity, so they keep the information away from adolescents
   d. many high schools in the United States do not offer sex education, or education about contraceptives
   e. all of the above

ADOLESCENCE

MATCHING

Mark the letter of the matching answer in the space provided beside each statement about health problems in adolescence.

__b__ 1. percentage of teenagers who decide to keep their babies after giving birth

__a__ 2. number of girls in the United States out of 1000, between the ages of 15 and 19, who get pregnant

__e__ 3. percentage of surveyed high school seniors who had drunk five or more drinks in within two weeks

__D__ 4. percentage of high school juniors and seniors who have tried marijuana

__C__ 5. percentage of high school seniors who regularly smoke cigarettes

__f__ 6. where most adolescents learn their alcoholic drinking habits

__h__ 7. adolescents are likely to use drugs if under pressure from this source

__i__ 8. tobacco leads to this kind of addiction

__J__ 9. marijuana leads to this kind of addiction

__K__ 10. this term refers to people who eat when they are depressed or anxious

a. 96
b. 94
c. 15
d. 40
e. 41
f. at home, from parents
g. at parties
h. peers
g. cultural norms
h. psychological problems
i. physical addiction
j. psychological addiction
k. emotional eaters
l. bulimia
m. early maturers
n. late maturers
o. girl friends and boy friends

ANSWERS TO THE SELF-TEST, CHAPTER 14

COMPLETION QUESTIONS

1. puberty (p. 368)
2. puberty (p. 368)
3. growth spurt (p. 369)
4. 12, 13, 18, 19 (p. 370)
5. 10, 11, 17, 18 (p. 370)
6. secondary (p. 371)
7. estradiol (p. 373)
8. adrenal androgen (p. 373)
9. image (p. 375)
10. early (p. 376)
11. 80, 70 (p. 378)
12. 11, 12, 6, 10 (p. 379)
13. 2 (p. 380)
14. parents, peers, books (p. 382)
15. 90 (p. 383)
16. heroin (p. 384)
17. attention, remember (p. 385)
18. physically (p. 385)
19. bulimia (p. 386)
20. anorexia nervosa (p. 380)

MULTIPLE CHOICE

1. a (p. 369)
2. d (p. 370)
3. d (p. 372)
4. e (pp. 373-374)
5. b (p. 374)
6. c (p. 374)
7. e (p. 377)
8. a (p. 378)
9. c (p. 379)
10. e (p. 381)

MATCHING

1. b (p. 381)
2. a (p. 380)
3. e (p. 383)
4. d (p. 384)
5. c (p. 385)
6. f (p. 383)
7. h (p. 384)
8. i (p. 385)
9. j (p. 385)
10. k (p. 385)

CHAPTER SUMMARY

Chapter 15 continues the section on <u>Adolescence</u> by discussing cognitive development of young people in adolescence, the ages from 10 to 19 years.

<u>Scientific and logical thought</u> characterizes the changes in adolescent's cognitions and capabilities as they leave childhood. A central development is adolescent's ability to conceive of the world as it might be, as opposed to the child's concrete conception of the world as it is. Another important feature of adolescent cognition is the ability to think in general, or abstract terms. Piaget recognized differences in the ways that children and adolescents solve problems. He suggested three distinctive qualities of adolescent thought: (1) ability to think of multiple possible solutions to a problem; (2) ability to hypothesize and deduce; and (3) ability to infer logical relations between abstract propositions. These qualities of scientific and logical thinking in adolescence are ingredients of formal operational thinking. <u>Levels of formal operational thought</u> describes the progression of thinking to the level of formal operations. The first level is thinking about multiple possibilities for solving a problem. The second level is systematic thought about which possibility is the most viable solution to a problem. Formal operational thinking is most likely to be used in situations and tasks that are familiar, simple and concrete, rather than in solving personal problems. Further, formal operational thinking is is more common among adolescents raised in technologically advanced cultures that emphasize scientific modes of thinking.

The section <u>Information processing</u> presents the view that adolescent thinking is not only more scientific and logical, but also characterized by expanded information processing capabilities. Adolescents can store more information in short-term memory than children can, which allows them to draw on more information for problem solving. Adolescent reasoning also benefits from their better planning abilities and greater knowledge about the content of formal and scientific problems.

<u>Achievement in school</u> is based on several important factors, including adolescents are taught in <u>school</u>, their <u>need to achieve</u> and fear of failure, <u>locus of control</u>, <u>gender</u>, and <u>family</u> characteristics. Locus of control refers to the adolescent's attributions for success and failure. Adolescents who believe that achievement is based on their own ability and effort --internal locus of control -- are more confident of their abilities, and are likely to succeed. Conversely, those who believe that causes of their achievement are beyond their control -- external locus of control -- are less confident about their

abilities, expect to fail, and are likely to do so. Differences in achievement are also observed between male and female adolescents. Males tend to outperform females in science and math, while females fare better in verbal tasks. Many factors contribute to these differences in achievement, including biology, experience, socialization, and motivation. The family affects adolescent achievement by providing financial, biological, environmental and motivational resources necessary for achievement.

Moral reasoning entails moral maturity, ideas and acts. Moral maturity increases during adolescence. The young adult is thus capable of making moral judgments based on personal values and standards, as opposed to externally imposed social conventions. Moral maturity results from the cognitive development of abstract reasoning abilities, psychological changes that make them question externally imposed rules, and social experiences that expose them to different moral positions and dilemmas. Lawrence Kohlberg's theory of moral development suggests that moral development progresses in stages. Mature moral reasoning is postconventional, which requires formal operational thought to think abstractly and weigh the relative merits of social conventions about right and wrong. While formal operational thought is necessary for postconventional moral reasoning, it is not sufficient. Moral ideas and moral acts do not always go hand-in-hand. Moral behavior is based on personal and situational factors, as well as the ability to think abstractly.

The chapter closes with a discussion of Adolescent egocentrism, that accompanies the physical, cognitive, social, and psychological changes in this period. Adolescents have an inflated view of their importance and uniqueness. There abstract reasoning abilities contribute to projections of what other persons, hypothetical or real, think of them. At first this is a problem, since the adolescents will have difficulty distinguishing the concerns of their imaginary audience from their own. Egocentrism may also lead young adolescents to imagine a personal fable of themselves, that is characterized by feelings of invincibility and uniqueness.

LEARNING OBJECTIVES

When you have finished studying Chapter 15 in both the text and this guide, you should be able to do the following:

1. Briefly discuss the difference between adolescents' and children's thinking.

2. Discuss the several distinctive qualities of thought discovered by Piaget.

3. Describe the development of formal operational thought in adolescence.

4. Discuss the factors that influence the development of formal operational thought.

5. Indicate how information processing capabilities improve during adolescence.

6. List the recommendations of educational researchers for improving the quality and quantity of instruction in high school so that students will achieve more.

7. Discuss the major personal factors that influence adolescent's achievement.

8. Discuss the various accounts and descriptions of moral maturity in adolescence that have been offered by psychologists.

9. Discuss the relation between moral thought and moral behavior.

10. Describe the major characteristics of adolescent egocentrism.

KEY TERMS

Interpropositional logic (p. 392)

Formal operational thinking (p. 392)

Need for achievement (p. 397)

Internal locus of control (p. 398)

External locus of control (p. 398)

Learned helplessness (p. 399)

ADOLESCENCE

Adolescent egocentrism (p. 403)

Imaginary audience (p. 403)

Personal fable (p. 403)

STUDY QUESTIONS

1. Describe the major qualities of adolescent thought noted by
   Piaget, and discuss how these qualities differ from
   children's thought. (pp. 390-393)

2. Compare "first order" thinking of children with the "second
   order" thinking of adolescents. (p. 392)

3. Discuss the changes in and characteristics of the different
   levels of formal operational thought in adolescence.
   (p. 393)

4. Discuss the evidence suggesting that formal operational
   thinking depends on experience, education, and situational
   factors. (p. 393)

5. How did Lesser and Paisner's study of a spiritual group of women challenge Piaget's conception of the link between logical and causal thinking? (p. 394)

6. How is information processing in adolescence more complete and thorough than in childhood? (p. 395)

7. Describe a typical school day for high school students. Include a description of attention patterns and problems. (p. 397)

8. How can the quality and quantity of high school instruction be improved? (p. 397)

9. What are the characteristics of underachievers? (pp. 397-398)

10. What personal factors influence achievement motivation? (pp. 397-398)

11. Define locus of control and discuss its role in achievement (pp. 398-399)

12. How do male and female adolescents differ in school achievement? (pp. 399-400)

13. What factors explain sex differences in achievement? (pp. 399-400)

14. Discuss the ways that family factors influence individual differences in achievement. (pp. 400-401)

15. Briefly discuss the reasons for differences in moral maturity between children and adolescents. (p. 401)

16. Why is formal operational thought necessary for postconventional moral reasoning? (p. 402)

17. Describe James Rest's model for integrating moral reasoning with moral actions. (pp. 402-403)

18. Define the concepts of adolescent egocentrism, imaginary audience, and personal fable. (p. 403)

19. How is the development of adolescent egocentrism related to the development of formal operational thought and perspective taking? (pp. 403-404)

SELF-TEST, CHAPTER 15

COMPLETION QUESTIONS

1. Adolescents can think in _general_ terms, linking past, present, and future events.

2. Piaget studied the development of adolescent thought by focusing on their understanding of _physical_ science.

3. Children's and adolescents' different problem solving strategies reflect differences in their _thought_ processes.

4. An adolescent's ability to think about the possible allows him or her to hypothesize and _deduce_ .

5. Piaget found that adolescents can think like _scientist_, separating variables, generating and testing hypotheses, and weighing probabilities.

6. Unlike children, adolescents can judge the truth of the logical relation between two _propositions_

7. Interpropositional logic is first possible in adolescence, and depends on _formal_ _operational_ thinking.

8. Thinking about propositions rather than objects is referred to as _2a_ - order thinking.

9. Formal operational thinking usually begins between the ages of _11_ and _15_ .

10. Mature formal operational thinkers search for necessary and _sufficient_ conditions when explaining physical events.

11. At the second level of formal operations thinking becomes _systematic_

12. Adolescents can keep more information in _short_ - term memory than children can.

13. Adolescents can select and _alter_ their information processing strategies better than children.

14. In a study of math skills of 5000 adolescents the best predictor of students' scores was the number of years of high school _algebra_ and _geometry_ they had taken.

15. Underachievers have little motivation to strive for success, or low _Need for achievement_.

16. Adolescents who attribute their achievement to luck have an _external_ locus of control.

17. Boys are likely to achieve more in school than girls, especially in the _physical_ sciences.

18. Middle-class adolescents have stronger academic abilities than poorer adolescents because of environmental and _genetic_ factors.

19. Psychologists who emphasize _cognitive_ development might say that moral maturity is being able to make moral judgments that are just and fair.

20. Adolescent _egocentrism_ makes adolescents think they are more important and unusual then they really are.

MULTIPLE CHOICE

1. Which is NOT typical of adolescent thought?

    a. think about the possible and the actual
    b. reason abstractly
    c. speculate
    d. first-order thinking
    e. hypothesize and make deductions

2. Adolescent thinking is like scientific thinking in which of the following ways?

    a. their ability to hypothesize
    b. their knowledge of statistics
    c. their ability to handle delicate scientific instruments
    d. their ability to test hypotheses by collecting evidence
    e. a and c only

3. Which of the following statements is FALSE?

    a. interpropositional logic is possible with formal operational thought
    b. abstract thought is characteristic of post-operational thinking
    c. the ability to speculate is characteristic of formal operational thinking
    d. abstract thought is characteristic of formal operational thinking
    e. none of the above

4. Circle all of the correct statements about levels of formal operational thought.

    a. thinking about alternative, hypotheses, and possibilities begins in early adolescence
    b. systematically thinking about possibilities does not begin until late adolescence
    c. mature formal operational thinkers stop working on a problem once they have found a single solution
    d. all adolescents use formal operational thinking
    e. young children cannot be trained to think in formal operational thought

5. Which of the following factors influences adolescents' achievement?

    a. number of years of high school algebra and geometry
    b. need for achievement
    c. personal standards for excellence
    d. fear of failing
    e. all of the above

6. Which of the following is NOT related to learned helplessness?

    a. believing nothing you do will make a difference
    b. believing you are not bright enough to solve a task
    c. internal locus of control for successes
    d. external locus of control for successes and failures
    e. expecting to fail

7. SAT scores in 1985 showed girls falling further behind boys in _____ as well as _____ and scientific tests.

    a. verbal; mathematical
    b. mathematical; spatial
    c. verbal; artistic
    d. analytic; mathematical
    e. reading; vocabulary

8. In a study by Kohlberg and Krebs on moral thought and honesty, a total of _____ percent of the preconventional reasoners cheated; only _____ percent of the postconventional reasoners cheated.

    a. 66; 75
    b. 50; 50
    c. 75; 66
    d. 100; 0
    e. 40; 60

MATCHING

Match the following terms with the statement that best defines
them.

_d_ 1. interpropositional logic
_h_ 2. formal operational thinking
_f_ 3. first-order thinking
_c_ 4. need for achievement
_a_ 5. internal locus of control
_e_ 6. external locus of control
_g_ 7. second-order thinking

a. belief that successes and failures are within one's
    personal control
b. fear of failure and test anxiety
c. desire and motivation to strive for success
d. ability to judge the truth of the logical relationship
    of propositions
e. belief that personal success and failure is determined by
    forces beyond one's control
f. thinking about objects
g. thinking about propositions
h. similar to scientific and logical thinking

ADOLESCENCE

ANSWERS TO THE SELF-TEST, CHAPTER 15

COMPLETION QUESTIONS

1. general (p. 390)
2. physical (p. 390)
3. thought (p. 390)
4. deduce (p. 391)
5. scientists (p. 391)
6. propositions (p. 392)
7. formal operational (p. 392)
8. first (p. 392)
9. 11, 15 (p. 393)
10. sufficient (p. 393)
11. systematic (p. 393)
12. short (p. 395)
13. plan (p. 395)
14. algebra, geometry (p. 396)
15. need for achievement (p. 397)
16. external (p. 398)
17. physical (p. 399)
18. genetic (p. 400)
19. cognitive (p. 401)
20. egocentrism (p. 403)

MULTIPLE CHOICE

1. d (pp. 390-392)
2. e (p. 391)
3. b (p. 392)
4. a, b (p. 393)
5. e (pp. 397-398)
6. c (pp. 398-399)
7. a (p. 400)
8. c (p. 402)

MATCHING

1. d (p. 392)
2. h (p. 392)
3. f (p. 392)
4. c (p. 397)
5. a (p. 398)
6. e (p. 398)
7. g (p. 392)

CHAPTER SUMMARY

The section Storms and stress discusses the different viewpoints
of researchers who describe the adolescent period. Clinicians
tend to see adolescence as a period of great stress, while other
researchers do not. Researchers generally agree, though, that
most adolescents experience fluctuations in moods. Most striking
is the rapidity with which adolescents change their moods.

Making transitions from childhood to early adolescence seems to
create much havoc for the young adolescent. Adolescents are
experiencing physical, cognitive and social changes at a rapid
rate. These changes bring on a host of worries about physical
appearance, about social issues, about peer acceptance and
relationships with members of the opposite sex. The challenges
of early adolescence can have negative affects on adolescents'
self-esteem, and fill them with self-doubt. The changes and
challenges of this erratic period of development may also
precipitate in an identity crisis. Erik Erikson suggested that
adolescents enter a period of psychosocial moratorium, in which
they focus much energy and attention on defining and finding
themselves. Gradually the adolescent will sort out the various
identity issues he or she faces concerning career, morality and
religion, political ideology, and social roles (including gender
roles). Those who successfully weather the storms and stresses
of adolescence reach a stage of identity achievement, while those
who don't are in a state of identity diffusion. Adolescents who
never experience an identity crisis are in a state of identity
foreclosure, and they generally plod through adolescence
accepting the identity that their parents have established for
them.

Family relationships are frequently strained for all involved
when a child enters adolescence. The adolescent is striving for
freedom and control at the same time that parents are attempting
to exert their control and influence over what the adolescent
thinks and does. Conflicts frequently arise between adolescents
and parents over issues like curfew times and doing chores,
rather than over sex, drugs, religion and politics. By late
adolescence family turmoil usually diminishes, and family
relationships generally improve once the adolescent leaves home.

There are individual differences in adolescents' relationships
with their parents. For example, sons' and daughters' conflicts
reveal interesting sex differences in adolescents' family
relationships. Girls tend to have more difficulty than boys in
asserting their independence while simultaneously keeping
emotionally close to their parents. Conflicts differ also.
Girls tend to argue with parents over emotional issues, whereas
boys argues over more practical issues. Parents' continuing

influence on their adolescent tends to be stable, reflecting the styles of discipline and communication they held during the adolescent's childhood. Moreover, parents' attitudes and behaviors are related to adolescents' self-image, competence, and confidence. While conflict seems inevitable between parents and adolescents, if the conflict is moderate the adolescent may benefit by developing autonomous and advanced moral thought. Serious conflict, though, can lead to many problems for the adolescent.

The section on peers versus parents discusses the amount of time adolescents spend with peers and family, and the resulting patterns of growth and conflict that this brings. Adolescents spend much enjoyable time with their peers, and tend to have less conflict with peers than with parents. Spending time with peers makes adolescents happy and supports their social development, but may also detract from their adjustment to school and to the social system. Conflict, conformity, and closeness are all issues of identity and relationships that emerge for adolescents as they move between the world of family and the world of friends. Adolescents feel closer to their peers than to their parents, tend to conform in both appearance and thought to their peers, and tend to rely on peers and parents differently for advice on various issues. By late adolescence (18 or 19 yearsold), most adolescents achieve true autonomy and make decisions on their own.

Peer relations usually consist of cliques of friends who are very similar to one another in age, race, and socioeconomic standing. When cliques join together for an activity (e.g., a football game) they form a crowd. Crowds generally have some common interest but are not linked by close friendship. Crowds serve different functions for adolescents and adults. For example, crowds can be controlled by school leaders, therefore establishing predictability and order in school settings, or crowds can influence adolescents' sense of identity and mold their self-concepts according to the norms and attitudes of the crowd. Cliques often provide a framework within which friendship and understanding develop. Within cliques there may be close peer dyads, their friendships are based on similarities, shared interests, empathy, understanding, and self-disclosure. Another form of peer relations that starts in adolescence is dating. Adolescent dating patterns depend on both their physical and psychological maturity, and serves many functions in adolescents' social development.

The discussion of adolescent problems presents recent research on the rates and potential causes of delinquency and suicide among adolescents. Most adolescents do not commit serious crimes. Those who do are likely to suffer from neurological and psychological problems that influence their delinquent behaviors. The rate of suicide among adolescents has increased dramatically in recent decade. More girls attempt suicide, but more boys succeed since they rely on more violent methods to achieve their ends.

Work has many positive influences on adolescent development. Many adolescents hold part-time jobs that seem to increase their responsibility, punctuality, and autonomy. On the other hand, adolescents who work may also spend less time with family and friends, and their school work may suffer. Regardless of work experience, adolescents are concerned with and start making decisions about their careers.

The final section of of the chapter discusses psychosocial maturity. The developmental tasks for adolescents are many, including learning how to maintain a regular schedule of daily activities and focusing on a limited course of development. All of these tasks must be mastered for the adolescent to perform behaviors that society requires of its functioning members.

LEARNING OBJECTIVES

When you have finished studying Chapter 16 in both the text and this guide, you should be able to do the following:

1. Describe the views of adolescent stress held by various researchers and clinicians.

2. Describe the difficulties encountered by children transitioning into early adolescence.

3. Discuss the search for identity in adolescence and individual differences in achieving identity.

4. Discuss the challenges adolescents face in attempting to establish autonomy without alienating themselves from their family.

5. Discuss the different ways that male and female adolescents relate to their family, noting especially the types of conflict encountered by each sex.

6. Describe the stability of parents' influence on their offspring from childhood through adolescence, noting how parental support affects adolescents' resolution of identity crises.

7. Describe the differences in adolescents' relations with peers versus parents.

8. Describe and explain the function of adolescent peer groups (i.e., cliques, friendships, and crowds).

9. Discuss how dating influences social and emotional development in adolescents.

10. Discuss the potential causes of delinquency.

11. Note the rates of adolescent suicide and how these have changed over time. Also discuss the potential causes of suicide.

12. Note the number of adolescents who hold part-time jobs. Discuss the possible advantages and disadvantages of employment for adolescent social and emotional development.

13. Describe the developmental tasks of adolescents (i.e., what adolescent must learn to function in society).

KEY TERMS

Storm and stress (p. 408)

Identity crisis (p. 412)

Psychosocial moratorium (p. 412)

Alienated identity achievement (p. 413)

Identity achievement (p. 413)

Identity diffusion (p. 414)

Identity moratorium (p. 414)

Identity foreclosure (p. 414)

Clique (p. 424)

Crowd (p. 424)

Juvenile delinquency (p. 427)

STUDY QUESTIONS

1.   Discuss the research findings on mood changes in adolescents. (pp. 408-409)

2.   Describe the stresses of adolescence. (pp. 408-409)

3.   Discuss the consequences of adolescents' physical, social, and cognitive growth in early adolescence. (p. 410)

4.   How is the self-esteem of young adolescents affected by the many changes and challenges they face? (pp. 411-412)

5. Define the following concepts and indicate how they relate to identity formation in adolescence: psychosocial moratorium, alienated identity achievement, identity achievement, identity diffusion, identity moratorium, identity foreclosure. (pp. 412-414)

6. How do adolescents reshape their relationships with their parents? (p. 415)

7. Describe the struggle for freedom and control between adolescents and their parents. (pp. 415-416)

8. How do sons' and daughters' conflicts with parents differ? (pp. 416-417)

9.   Describe the research by Roberts and colleagues attesting to the stability of parents' styles of disciplining and communicating with their children. (p. 419)

10. How do parents' attitudes and behaviors influence adolescents' self-esteem and identity? (pp. 419-421)

11. How do adolescents spend time together, and how does this affect their relationships with their parents? (pp. 421-422)

12. Adolescents' relationships with their friends differ from those with their parents. Discuss these differences regarding conflict, conformity, closeness, and the kinds of problems discussed with peers versus parents. (pp. 422-424)

13. What is the function of cliques for adolescents? (pp. 424-425)

14. What is the function of crowds for adults supervising
adolescents? (pp. 424-425)

15. Describe the quality of adolescent friendships.
(pp. 425-426)

16. What factors influence adolescent dating patterns? (p. 426)

17. What function does dating serve for adolescents?
(pp. 426-427)

18. Describe the kinds of crimes juvenile delinquents engage in,
and the contributing factors to delinquent behavior.
(pp. 427-430)

19. What are the potential causes of adolescent suicide?
    (pp. 430-432)

20. What are the beneficial and harmful psychological,
    social, and academic outcomes associated with
    adolescent working? (p. 433)

21. What are the developmental tasks that must be accomplished
    for adolescents to reach psychosocial maturity?
    (pp. 434-436)

ADOLESCENCE

SELF-TEST, CHAPTER 16

COMPLETION QUESTIONS

1. G. Stanley Hall and Anna Freud characterized adolescence as a period of _Stress_ and _Storm_ .

2. Although some adolescents experience more stress than others, almost all adolescents are subject to _mood_ fluctuations.

3. Young adolescents are most likely to feel unhappy and have low self-esteem if they are experiencing _stress_ from several sources.

4. _Erik Erikson_ theorized that adolescence is a crisis among crises.

5. The many challenges to adolescents' sense of self may precipitate an _identity_ crisis.

6. Erikson suggested that adolescents enter a period of psychosocial _moratorium_ when their main task is to find themselves and establish their role and niche in society.

7. Adolescents who do not want to follow the standards offered by society have developed an _alienated_ identity achievement.

8. Adolescents with a unified self-image, who can function adequately and successfully in society have reached a stage of identity _achievement_.

9. Adolescents who remain uncommitted and hold fast to their childhood are in a state of identity _diffusion_.

10. Adolescents who are still searching for a unified self-image, yet who have not committed themselves firmly to a career or a political or religious view, are in a state of identity _moratorium_.

11. Adolescents who do not search for identity, have never experienced a sense of crisis, and accept the identity that their parents established for them are in a state of identity _foreclosure_.

12. Adolescents want freedom and autonomy in their family relationships. This frequently causes conflict, whereas parents want to _control_ what the adolescent thinks and does.

13. In childhood, it is _____*males*_____ who most often have problems, while _____*female*_____-sexed adolescents are most likely to have problems.

14. Parents are most restrictive with their _____*female*_____-sexed adolescents.

15. Female adolescents are likely to have conflicts over _____*emotional*_____ issues, and males are likely to have conflicts over practical issues with their parents.

16. Parenting styles tend to be _____*stable*_____ as the children develop from childhood into adolescence.

17. Standing on the roof of a car and trying to stay on while the car goes around corners is called _____*Car*_____ *Surfing*.

18. Small groups of young adolescent friends of the same sex are known as _____*Cliques*_____.

19. The rate of suicide among adolescents has increased _____*300*_____ percent in the last 30 years.

MULTIPLE CHOICE

1. Which of the following researchers did NOT believe that adolescence was necessarily a period of storm and stress?

    a. G. Stanley hall
    b. Anna Freud
    c. Margaret Mead
    d. Erik Erikson
    e. none of the above

2. Which of the following statements about adolescents' moods is FALSE?

    a. adolescents experience frequent changes in mood
    b. adolescents' moods change rapidly
    c. adolescents' moods are extreme
    d. adolescents' extreme moods last longer than adults' extreme moods
    e. adolescents get into more emotional situations than adults do

3. Which of the following statements about early adolescence
    is TRUE?

    a. physical, social, and psychological changes can create
       stress for young adolescents
    b. issues of independence may become critical at home
    c. family disputes are not common in early adolescence, but
       become common after ninth grade
    d. a and b only
    e. a and c only

4. Adolescents who do not search for identity, do not
    experiment with roles or experience an identity crisis, and
    assume an identity that their parents have set for them,
    are in a state of:

    a. identity foreclosure
    b. identity diffusion
    c. identity achievement
    d. alienated identity achievement
    e. identity moratorium

5. Which of the following statements about sons' and daughters'
    conflicts is FALSE?

    a. boys are tend to get into conflicts with parents over
       emotional issues
    b. parents try to keep their adolescent boys at home to
       prevent them from getting their girl friends pregnant
    c. girls are more likely than boys to argue for access to
       the family car keys
    d. parents give sons less room to maneuver than they give
       daughters
    e. all of the above

6. Which of the following statements about parents' influence
    on adolescents is FALSE?

    a. adolescents do not feel the influence of their parents
       once they have left the period of childhood
    b. the degree of control parents exert on their children
       remains stable from childhood through adolescence
    c. parents are likely to stress achievement more for their
       13-year-olds than for their 3-year-olds
    d. parents express less physical affection with their
       13-year-olds than with their 3-year-olds
    e. how adolescents think about themselves is related to
       their parents' attitudes and behavior

7. Although spending time with friends makes adolescents happy
    and supports their social development, research has shown
    that adolescents who spend the most time with their friends
    have the following problems:

    a. never develop a mature identity
    b. abuse their parents
    c. wide mood swings and problems in school
    d. none of the above
    e. all of the above

8. Which of the following statements about juvenile delinquency
    is TRUE?

    a. most adolescents do things that they know are wrong
    b. the most serious offenses adolescents are charged with
       usually are related to theft
    c. boys are more likely to be delinquent than girls
    d. for both girls and boys, delinquency peaks at around age
       15
    e. all of the above

9. Adolescents who attempt or commit suicide have which of the
    following characteristics?

    a. accident prone
    b. see things in black and white, and view bad situations
       as hopeless
    c. like taking drugs
    d. unattractive
    e. likely to seek help from others when problems occur

10. Which of the following statements about adolescents who
    work is FALSE?

    a. they develop a sense of responsibility
    b. they are dependable
    c. they are punctual
    d. they are self-reliant
    e. they enjoy school more

ADOLESCENCE

MATCHING

A. For each of the following statements indicate whether they are more likely to apply to male or to female adolescents, or to both

_c/a_ 1. inhabit female-dominated environments
_a_ 2. base their emerging identities on their ability to get along with other people
_b_ 3. spend less time with their families and more time at school, at work, or engaged in hobbies and sports
_a_ 4. parents worry whether they are safe on their own, and they worry about their sexual behavior
_a_ 5. have a hard time coming to terms with their independence
_a_ 6. have more conflicts with parents, especially their mothers
_a_ 7. attempt suicide
_b_ 8. succeed at suicide
_b_ 9. use violent methods when attempting suicide
_b_ 10. hold a part-time job
_c_ 11. be a member of a clique and conform to its culture
_c_ 12. spend a lot of time with friends

a. more likely to apply to female adolescents
b. more likely to apply to male adolescents
c. likely to apply to both males and females

B. Match the following terms with their definition.

_c_ 1. alienated identity achievement
_d_ 2. identity achievement
_b_ 3. identity diffusion
_a_ 4. identity foreclosure

a. never experience an identity crisis
b. remain uncommitted, have trouble making decisions, lack direction or interest in academic, political, or social questions
c. show a marked change in identity, which is marked by a rejection of the standard values established by society and their parents
d. successfully establish a unified self-image
e. have no task more important than finding themselves
f. actively looking for a way to commit themselves to meaningful work or political views

ANSWERS TO THE SELF-TEST, CHAPTER 16

COMPLETION QUESTIONS

1. storm, stress (p. 408)
2. mood (p. 408)
3. stress (p. 411)
4. Erik Erikson (p. 412)
5. identity (p. 412)
6. moratorium (p. 412)
7. alienated (p. 413)
8. achievement (p. 413)
9. diffusion (p. 414)
10. moratorium (p. 414)
11. foreclosure (p. 414)
12. control (p. 415)
13. males, female (p. 416)
14. female (p. 416)
15. emotional (p. 417)
16. stable (p. 419)
17. car surfing (p. 422)
18. cliques (p. 424)
19. 300 (p. 431)

MULTIPLE CHOICE

1. c (p. 408)
2. d (p. 409)
3. d (p. 410)
4. a (p. 414)
5. e (pp. 416-417)
6. a (p. 419)
7. c (p. 422)
8. e (pp. 427-428)
9. b (p. 432)
10. e (p. 433)

MATCHING

A.

1. c (p. 416)
2. a (p. 416)
3. b (p. 416)
4. a (p. 416)
5. a (p. 417)
6. a (p. 417)
7. a (p. 431)
8. b (p. 431)
9. b (p. 431)
10. b (p. 433)
11. c (p. 424)
12. c (p. 421)

B.

1. c (p. 413)
2. d (p. 413)
3. b (p. 414)
4. a (p. 414)

CHAPTER SUMMARY

Chapter 17 begins the section on Early and middle adulthood by
discussing physical development. The age boundaries of this
group are not as clearly marked as for younger people,
especially since there are wider individual variations among
older adults than among young people. The section on the adult
body explains these differences with the principle of
"increased differentiation" in development in older people. One
common fact in the physical development of adults is that aging
does not progress uniformly: some physical systems deteriorate
faster than others. An important distinction is made between
the effects of primary or normal aging and secondary aging on
the bodily systems. While primary aging is mainly a function
of biology and genes, secondary aging is more related to
disease, physical abuse and disuse, and environmental factors.
It is not always clear whether changes in bodily systems and
appearance are a product of primary or secondary aging.

Many noticeable changes in appearance result from aging.
Predominant among these are changes in skin from smooth and
taut to wrinkled and slack, and changes in hair texture,
color, and quantity. Gray hair, for example, is one of the
most reliable indicators of aging, as is balding in men.
Aging also slows the growth of nails, though diet, general
health, hormone levels, blood supply, and environmental
conditions also affect the growth and appearance of nails.
Aging also produces changes in the quality of muscle cells
-- they atrophy and die -- and the proportion of fat cells
to muscle cells increases.

Changes also occur in adult sensory systems. In general, the
senses become less responsive to external stimulations, but not
to the point of interfering with everyday functioning until late
adulthood. Internally aging affects the cardiovascular system,
the heart, the respiratory system, the endocrine system,
and the reproductive system. In particular, aging has the
following affects: (a) the cells within the cardiovascular system
cannot divide and reproduce themselves, which results in a less
efficient cardiovascular system; (b) the heart muscle weakens,
pumping less blood and at a slower rate; (c) the lungs take in
less air, and more residual air stays in the lungs; and (d) the
secretion of hormones from the endocrine system is slowed, cells
in various parts of the body are less responsive to hormones, the
chemical messengers that carry hormonal messages into cells are
changed, and the levels of enzymes that respond to hormones are
changed. The effects of aging in the endocrine system are
complex, since the endocrine glands -- pituitary, parathyroid,
thyroid, pancreas, thymus, and adrenal glands -- regulate
many functions, such as sexual reproduction, immunity, metabolism,
growth, and the aging of cells.

ADULTHOOD

Aging has different affects on the reproductive systems of men
and women. The male reproductive system functions less quickly
and efficiently. This is partly due to an aging endocrine
system, since this system is interdependent with the
reproductive system. Men's testes produce less sperm as they
continue to age. Likewise, the female reproductive system
produces different levels of hormones, creating changes in her
fertility and vagina. During their forties women's menstrual
periods get shorter and more irregular, signaling the "change
of life." Typically by the age of 50 a woman's menstruation
stops completely, and she has reached menopause. At that point
her body's production of estrogen and progesterone declines
sharply. One result of the decline in estrogen levels is that
the muscle walls of the vagina grow thin and less elastic, and
the walls also produce fewer normal secretions, making the vagina
feel dryer.

The section on sexuality indicates that early and middle adulthood
may well be the sexual prime of life. When couples first live
together or marry their rates of sexual intercourse typically are
the highest of their adult lives. Not long after, the rate of
intercourse gradually declines. Although physiological changes in
sexual responsiveness does not preclude adults from enjoying sex,
there may be biological, sociological and psychological reasons for
a decline in the frequency of intercourse with age.

LEARNING OBJECTIVES

When you have finished studying Chapter 14 in both the text and
this guide, you should be able to do the following:

1. Describe what researchers mean when they say that the
   development of older people becomes more differentiated than
   development among younger people.

2. Discuss the major noticeable changes in appearance due to
   aging among early and middle aged adults.

3. Describe the changes in proportion of fat to muscle in
   developing adults.

4. Discuss the changes in adult sensory systems, noting the
   ways that adults can adapt to these changes.

5. Describe the cardiovascular system and the affects of aging
   on this system and the heart muscle.

6. Compare the respiratory functioning of young adults with
   older adults, noting changes in lung capacity.

7. List the various glands and their functions in the endocrine system.

8. Note the general affects of aging on the endocrine system.

9. Describe the affects of aging on the male and female reproductive system, respectively.

10. Discuss the changes in adult sexual behaviors following marriage or co-habitation.

11. Discuss the possible reasons for the declining frequency of intercourse that accompanies aging.

KEY TERMS

Primary (normal) aging (p. 443)

Secondary aging (p. 443)

Vellus hair (p. 444)

Terminal hair (p. 444)

Pattern baldness (p. 444)

Cardiac output (p. 447)

Climacteric (p. 455)

Menopause (p. 455)

STUDY QUESTIONS

1. Compare the rate and extent of the physical changes in adulthood with the physical changes in young people. (pp. 442-443)

2. What is the difference between primary and secondary aging? (p. 443)

3. Discuss the individual differences in people's psychological response to aging. How do cultural differences influence individual responses? (p. 443)

4. How does aging affect the color, texture, and quantity of people's hair? (pp. 443-444)

5. Describe pattern baldness in men and discuss its cause. (pp. 443-444)

6.   How does aging affect the growth and appearance of skin and
     nails? (pp. 444-445)

7.   What factors other than aging affect the growth and
     appearance of skin and nails (i.e., secondary aging)?
     (p. 445)

8.   How does the make-up of muscles change with age?
     (p. 445)

9.   How does the proportion of fat cells to muscle cells change
     as a result of aging and exercise? (p. 445)

10. Briefly list the changes in vision that occur in early and
     middle adulthood. (p. 445)

ADULTHOOD

11. How does aging affect the hearing of men? Of women?
    (p. 446)

12. Describe the cardiovascular system and changes in this
    system resulting from primary and secondary aging.
    (pp. 446-447)

13. Why does cardiac output decline with age? (p. 447)

14. Older people take in less breath in a single breath than
    younger people, yet their lung capacity is the same.
    How does this affect the residual volume of air in older
    people? (p. 447)

15. List the various glands that comprise the endocrine system.
    (pp. 449-453)

16. Describe the functions of the endocrine system and its various glands. (pp. 449-453)

17. How does aging affect the endocrine system? (pp. 449-453) (pp. 449-453)

18. Discuss the affects of aging on the male reproductive system. (pp. 453-454)

19. Discuss the affects of aging on the female reproductive system. (pp. 454-455)

20. Describe the stereotype and truth about menopausal women? (p. 455)

ADULTHOOD

21. How do the sexual experiences of adults differ from those of
     adolescents? (pp. 455-456)

22. How does sexual activity change from early to middle
     adulthood? (pp. 455-458)

23. How do couples cope with male erectile problems?
     (pp. 456-458)

SELF-TEST, CHAPTER 17

COMPLETION QUESTIONS

1. The greater number of individual variations in development among older adults is referred to as _____.

2. Aging rarely progresses uniformly, rather some physical systems continue to function well, while others _____.

3. In cultures where aging is revered, the physical signs of aging may enhance self-confidence and _____.

4. Fine, short, and colorless hair is called _____ hair.

5. Coarse, longer, colored hair is called _____ hair.

6. Men inherit a form of baldness, called _____ baldness, that starts at the temples, moves across the top of the scalp, and finally leaves a fringe of terminal hair.

7. After menopause, women may find that their bodies' lower levels of sex hormones cause their pubic hair to thin or to _____.

8. The nails of an 80-year-old may grow _____ percent slower than those of a young person.

9. By middle age, many people need _____ to read or to perform other activities up close.

10. Although the size and weight of the pituitary do not change with age, the _____ supply to it gradually decreases after puberty.

11. The adrenal glands release hormones that mediate the response to _____.

12. The pancreas produces the hormone _____, which is needed to metabolize the sugars in the diet.

13. The _____ gland sits in the upper chest cavity and plays an important role in the immune system.

14. The testes of adult men between the age of 20 and 39 produce sperm in _____ percent of the sperm-producing tubules; after the age of 80 men produce sperm in only _____ percent of the tubules.

ADULTHOOD

15. Compared to that of a 20-year-old, it takes the penis of a 50-year-old _____ times longer to grow fully erect.

16. By the time a man is 60, the angle of his fully erect penis is _____ degrees.

17. The "change of life" for women approaching menopause is also known as _____.

18. Menstruation stops in women when they have reached _____.

19. Sudden, irreversible erectile problems are not common in middle-aged men, but fears of _____ are.

20. The aging male's gradual decline in the sex hormone _____ explains part of his decline in sexual activity.

MULTIPLE CHOICE

1. Which of the following is not related to secondary aging?

   a. physical abuse
   b. genetics
   c. physical disuse
   d. disease
   e. overexposure to sunlight

2. Which of the following is the most reliable physical indicator of aging?

   a. gray hair
   b. wrinkles
   c. terminal hair
   d. pattern baldness
   e. vellus hair

3. Which of the following statements about the affects of aging on muscle and fat is FALSE?

   a. until about the age of 39 people's muscles grow increasingly dense
   b. after the age of 39 muscles begin to shrink
   c. muscles atrophy when they are not used
   d. with aging, as muscle cells die, fat cells increase
   e. none of the above

4. Which of the following statements about the affects of aging
   on hearing is FALSE?

   a. hearing declines slowly after the mid-twenties
   b. older men are likely to lose the ability to hear sounds
      at high frequencies
   c. older men are more likely to hear the sound of a ringing
      doorbell than older women
   d. there are wide individual differences in hearing loss
   e. speech sounds such as -s, -z, -f, and -g may eventually
      become inaudible

5. Unlike bone and muscle cells, the cells within the
   cardiovascular system:

   a. are not elastic and thick
   b. become thin and dry
   c. are replaced by fat cells
   d. cannot divide and reproduce
   e. cannot retain water

6. Compared to younger people, older people retain a higher
   residual volume of air in their lungs because:

   a. older people take in smaller breaths in a single breath
   b. older people and younger people have the same lung
      capacity
   c. young people are less likely to smoke than older people
   d. both a and b
   e. none of the above

7. Which of the following is NOT part of the endocrine system?

   a. pituitary
   b. kidney
   c. thyroid
   d. pancreas
   e. adrenal

8. The endocrine system regulates which of the following
   functions?

   a. sexual reproduction
   b. immunity to stress and disease
   c. metabolism
   d. growth and the aging of cells
   e. all of the above

ADULTHOOD

9.　Which of the following statements is FALSE?

　　a. the pituitary's follicle-stimulating hormone (FSH)
　　　 and luteinizing hormone (LH) regulate the hormone
　　　 production of the male testes
　　b. FSH must be present for sperm to mature
　　c. FSH must be present for the testes to produce
　　　 testosterone
　　d. as the bloodstream fills with testosterone, the
　　　 pituitary slows the production of LH
　　e. LH must be present for the testes to produce
　　　 testosterone

10.　Androgens are sometimes called "male" hormones because:

　　a. only men have androgens
　　b. females stop producing androgens after puberty
　　c. compared to females, males have a greater amount of
　　　 androgens than estrogen and progesterone
　　d. males produce androgens before females
　　e. all of the above

MATCHING

Match the gland of the endocrine system with its function.

　_____　1.　pituitary
　_____　2.　parathyroid
　_____　3.　pancreas
　_____　4.　adrenal
　_____　5.　thymus
　_____　6.　thyroid

a. secretes hormones that help the body to metabolize minerals
　 such as calcium and phosphates
b. known as the master gland of the endocrine system; secretes
　 growth hormone, influences the metabolism, growth, and
　 repair of cells
c. releases the hormones epinephrine and norepinephrine into
　 the bloodstream, which mediate the response to stress
d. produces insulin, which stimulates the carrying of blood
　 sugar to the cells of the body
e. produces T cells, which play a role in the immune system by
　 rejecting foreign cells and tumors
f. releases hormones that regulate the body's metabolism of fats
　 and carbohydrates, regulate the bones' absorption of calcium
　 and phosphate, and stimulate the cell' use of oxygen

ANSWERS TO THE SELF-TEST, CHAPTER 17

COMPLETION QUESTIONS

1. differentiation (p. 442)
2. deteriorate(p. 442)
3. self-esteem (p. 443)
4. vellus (p. 444)
5. terminal (p. 444)
6. pattern (p. 444)
7. disappear (p. 444)
8. 38 (p. 445)
9. glasses (p. 445)
10. blood (p. 450)
11. stress (p. 451)
12. insulin (p. 451)
13. thymus (p. 452)
14. 90, 10 (p. 454)
15. 6 (p. 454)
16. 45 (p. 454)
17. climacteric (p. 455)
18. menopause (p. 455)
19. impotence (p. 456)
20. testosterone (p. 456)

MULTIPLE CHOICE

1. b (p. 443)
2. a (p. 444)
3. e (p. 445)
4. c (p. 446)
5. d (p. 447)
6. d (p. 447)
7. b (p. 450)
8. e (p. 449)
9. c (pp. 453-454)
10. c (pp. 454-455)

MATCHING

1. b (p. 449)
2. a (p. 451)
3. d (p. 451)
4. c (p. 451)
5. e (p. 452)
6. f (p. 451)

CHAPTER SUMMARY

Chapter 18 continues the section on <u>Early and middle adulthood</u> by discussing cognitive development of adults in this age group. This chapter also includes information on cognitive development in late adulthood for comparison purposes.

The section on <u>The information-processing system</u> discusses the scant findings on adult cognition and highlights some of the shortcomings of this research. Cognition, learning, and remembering for all ages relies upon information-processing systems to transfer and manipulate information. Although learning (acquiring information) and remembering (storing and retrieving information) abilities are fairly stable until old age, young adults fare better in their cognitive performance on experimental tasks. These apparent age changes in cognition may reflect underlying cohort effects or research design problems. Cohort effects may result from several educational advantages that young adults have over older adults. For example, young adults today have more years of formal education, have much more recent practice in the kinds of skills required in laboratory experiments, and may have different educational experiences than older adults. In addition, research may be designed to tap the cognitive skills that are more relevant to younger than to older adults. Laboratory experiments are unlikely to test learning and memory for everyday situations, or to present information in a familiar context. Thus, while older adults do not test as well as young adults under laboratory conditions, they may perform better under everyday conditions. Indeed, research has suggested that when older adults are presented information in a personally meaningful context for learning and remembering, they function as well as young adults.

Human memory is presented in two sections: <u>short-term memory</u> and <u>long-term memory</u>. Short-term memory has a very limited storage capacity, and information may remain in short-term memory for up to 15 seconds. Adults' short-term memory capacity and speed remain fairly stable until around the age of 60. Information from short-term memory must be encoded into long-term memory in order to retrieve it later. Young adults are more efficient than older adults at encoding information into long-term memory and retrieving it. Both young and old adults are assumed to have infinite long-term memory capacities, yet older people may fail to use the memory strategies that younger people use spontaneously. Young and older adults seem to organize information about events (episodic memories), and about related facts and concepts (i.e., semantic memories), in similar ways. Research has shown that episodic memories, but not semantic memories, may be affected by aging. Research has also suggested that memory for pictures seems stronger in both older and young adults than memory for words, and ability to recognize declines less than their ability to recall information.

Factors that may influence memory include the conditions under which information is encoded into and retrieved from memory, as well as the characteristics of the people under study (e.g., IQ). The section on memory strategies indicates than older adults can improve their memories by using memory strategies that elaborate on information or move it to a deeper level of cognitive processing. Encoding strategies include: (1) organizing information by category; (2) using verbal aids, or mnemonic deices; (3) creating a vivid mental image of items to be remembered; and (4) systematically rehearsing the information to be remembered. Older adults may not use these strategies as spontaneously as young adults do, possibly because they are less motivated or have less energy available for processing information at a deep level. In addition, young people seem to have a capacity surplus that allows them to pick up extra information, even when they are not intending to do so. Although young people are advantaged in information pick-up, encoding, and retrieval, older adults appear to have a better understanding of how memory works, or metamemory.

The section on Intellectual abilities focuses on two basic types of intelligence: fluid and crystallized. Fluid intelligence is required for the identification and comprehension of relationships and the drawing of inferences out of that comprehension. Research has indicated that fluid intelligence remains stable until late adulthood. Crystallized intelligence refers to acquired knowledge and intellectual skills and to the sum of a person's quantitative thinking, judgment, and wisdom. Crystallized intelligence influences a person's application of fluid intelligence within specific social and cultural contexts. Any loss in fluid intelligence, up to the age of 65, is countered by a comparable gain in crystallized intelligence.

Reasoning and problem solving skills also remain fairly stable until late adulthood. Some researchers believe that older adults reach an even higher level of cognitive competence than suggested by Piaget's theory of cognitive development. According to Piaget, cognitive maturity is attained in adolescence, with the acquisition of formal operations. However, older adults have more experience with solving everyday, practical problems that require concrete thought. Therefore, they become more adept at applying experience, knowledge, and wisdom to everyday problems. The ability for older people to solve everyday problems -- which usually have uncertain outcomes -- more effectively than young people, is related to their greater breadth of experience and their realistic understanding of the problems. Other researchers have suggested that adults may use formal thought to enhance their everyday cognitions and understandings of the concrete world. Older adults' use of <u>dialectical reasoning</u> to make sense of the world may be a step beyond the developmental level of formal operational thinking.

The chapter ends with a discussion of <u>problem-solving skills</u>, <u>concept formation</u>, and <u>expertness</u> among adults. In general, young and middle-aged adults outperform older adults in experimental problem-solving tasks, have more efficient methods of organizing knowledge about certain subjects, and are better at developing proficiency in new areas of knowledge. However, older adults do gain expert understanding of one or two areas as they gain experience and competence in those areas.

LEARNING OBJECTIVES

When you have finished studying Chapter 15 in both the text and this guide, you should be able to do the following:

1. Describe the changes, or lack of changes, in learning and memory abilities during adulthood.

2. Discuss what is meant by information-processing, especially as it relates to cognition, learning, and memory.

3. Discuss how older adults compare with young adults on experimental tests of cognitive ability.

4. Discuss the factors that influence different performance outcomes for young and old adults on experimental tests of cognitive ability.

5. Indicate how information processing capabilities decline during adulthood.

6. Describe the various components of memory.

7. Discuss how information is encoded into long-term memory.

8. Briefly compare the short- and long-term memory capacities of young adults with older adults.

9. Define episodic memory and semantic memory.

11. Discuss the factors that influence information encoding and retrieval from memory.

12. List and briefly describe the strategies that enhance memory.

13. Describe the differences between older and young adults in their use of memory strategies.

14. Define metamemory.

15. Note the possible reasons that older adults sometimes fail to use effective memory strategies.

16. Discuss the factors that influence adults' intellectual performance.

17. Define fluid intelligence and crystallized intelligence.

18. Discuss the changes in fluid intelligence and crystallized intelligence that occur during adulthood.

19. Discuss how older adults' "realistic understanding" may be more adaptive than formal operational thought for everyday problem solving.

20. Define dialectical reasoning.

21. Compare the problem-solving skills of young and old adults.

22. Compare the concept formation skills of young and old adults.

23. Describe how expertise in an area of knowledge enables older adults to master that area.

KEY TERMS

Sensory memory (p. 465)

Long-term memory (p. 466)

Episodic memories (p. 467)

Semantic memories (p. 467)

Metamemory (p. 469)

Fluid intelligence (p. 471)

Crystallized intelligence (p. 471)

Dialectical reasoning (p. 474)

STUDY QUESTIONS

1. How might differences in cognitive performance of old and
    young adults be explained by cohort effects? (pp. 462-463)

2. How might differences in cognitive performance of old and
    young adults be explained by they way experiments
    are designed? (pp. 462-465)

3. How does the content and context of laboratory-based tests
    of cognition affect the performance of older adults?
    (pp. 464-465)

ADULTHOOD

4.   Describe how information is processed at the different
      levels of memory, and eventually encoded into long-term
      memory for later retrieval. (pp. 465-466)

5.   What happens to short-term memory during adulthood?
      (p. 466)

6.   How does long-term memory differ from short-term memory?
      (pp. 466-467)

7.   How is information organized in long-term memory? (p. 467)

8.   How does aging affect people's episodic memories and
      semantic memories? (p. 467)

9. Note the factors that affect encoding and retrieval of information from memory. (p. 468)

10. What are the memory strategies that young adults are more likely to spontaneously employ to enhance their memory? (p. 468)

11. What is metamemory? (p. 469)

12. Discuss the various explanations of why older adults sometimes fail to use effective memory strategies. (pp. 469-470)

13. How might factors that interfere with laboratory learning be adaptive for adult learning in the real world? (pp. 470-471)

14. Briefly discuss the factors related to adults' intellectual performance. (p. 471)

15. Define fluid intelligence and crystallized intelligence. (p. 471)

16. How does the development of fluid intelligence differ from that of crystallized intelligence? (pp. 471-473)

17. How might developmental gains in crystallized intelligence counter the effects of losses in fluid intelligence? (pp. 472-473)

18. Why do older adults generally make better decisions about everyday situations that have uncertain outcomes? (pp. 473-474)

19.   What is dialectical reasoning? (p. 474)

20.   How do older adults compare with young adults in their
      problem-solving skills and concept-formation skills?
      (pp. 474-475)

21.   Describe expertness, and its advantages and disadvantages,
      in adulthood. (pp. 475-476)

SELF-TEST, CHAPTER 15

COMPLETION QUESTIONS

1. Through most of adulthood, the information-processing system remains relatively _stable_, and may even continue to improve in efficiency, in some cases.

2. Adult cognition generally starts declining after the age of ~~seventy~~ or _70_.

3. Learning and remembering rely on cognitive processes that _transfer_ information.

4. Learning and remembering change little during adulthood, at least until _old_ age.

5. _age_ itself is not a very good predictor of adults' abilities to learn or to remember.

6. The fact that young adults have higher average scores on experimental tests of cognitive ability than older adults, may result from _cohort_ effects and research _____.

7. _Sensory_ memory records information quite close to the time and form of the perception.

8. Sensory memory decays after _1_ second(s), unless it is processed to the next level of memory.

9. Information remains in the limited storage of short-term memory for up to _15_ seconds.

10. By applying memory strategies, information may be transferred from short-term to _long_ -term memory for later retrieval.

11. Encoding and retrieval processes move information between long-term and _short_ -term memory stores.

12. Older adults have more difficulty dividing their _attention_ between two tasks.

13. _short_ -term memory seems to slow down as people age.

14. Short-term memory has the capacity to retain up to _7_ numbers.

15. Memory for events, or things that happen to us, linked to specific times and places, is known as _episodic_ memory.

16. Memories that are organized around related facts and concepts are known as _Semantic_ memories.

17. Older adults are less efficient at _encoding_ information into long-term memory as well as at retrieving it.

18. Memory for _images/pictures_ seems stronger than memory for words.

19. In general, people's ability to _recall_ information declines more than their ability to recognize information.

20. Understanding how memory works is known as _metamory_.

21. _Fluid_ intelligence is required for the identification and comprehension of relationships and the drawing of inferences out of that comprehension.

22. _Crystallized_ intelligence corresponds to acquired knowledge.

23. Adults who use dialectical reasoning may be thinking at a level higher than Piaget's highest level of cognitive maturity known as _formal_ thought.

MULTIPLE CHOICE

1. Which of the following explains the differences in cognitive performance between older and young adults in laboratory-based experiments?

   a. quantity of formal education of young and old adults
   b. recency of practice in the kinds of skills tested
   c. quality of educational experience of old and young adults
   d. the kind of information being tested
   e. all of the above

2. Which of the following factors will enhance the performance of older adults in laboratory-based tests of cognitive abilities?

   a. using testing materials that are familiar to the learner
   b. testing in a context that is familiar
   c. using an experimenter who is older than the subjects
   d. only a and b
   e. a, b, and c

ADULTHOOD

3. A father's memory of his daughter's high school graduation
   is an example of:

   a. semantic memory
   b. short-term memory
   c. recognition
   d. episodic memory
   e. sensory memory

4. A person who tries to remember the face of a person who
   mugged her by creating an vivid image of the mugger is
   using:

   a. a mnemonic device
   b. a memory strategy
   c. her short-term memory
   d. a verbal aid to memory
   e. systematic rehearsal

5. Which of the following is NOT a reason for older adults'
   tendency to fail to use effective memory strategies?

   a. they have less energy available for processing
      information
   b. they have a capacity surplus
   c. they cannot or will not apply themselves to the
      demands of deeply processing information
   d. they may not have the relevant information about memory
      strategies for learning
   e. none of the above

6. Which of the following factors are related to adults'
   intellectual performance?

   a. social status
   b. educational levels
   c. IQ
   d. fluid and crystallized intelligence
   e. all of the above

7. A person who constantly seeks to integrate and order his or
   her understanding of life, and sees the universe as a
   continuous, ongoing process, is engaging in:

   a. meditation
   b. formal operational thought
   c. dialectical reasoning
   d. concrete thought
   e. realistic understanding

MATCHING

Mark the following as more true for older adults or more true for young adults

_a_ 1. expert in a single area of knowledge
_b_ 2. likely to develop proficiency in new areas of knowledge
_b_ 3. do well in laboratory experiments test of memory
_a_ 4. have a strong understanding of how memory works
_b_ 5. have many years of formal education

a. more true for older adults
b. more true for young adults

ADULTHOOD

ANSWERS TO THE SELF-TEST, CHAPTER 18

COMPLETION QUESTIONS

1. stable (p. 462)
2. 70 (p. 462)
3. transfer (p. 462)
4. old (p. 462)
5. age (p. 462)
6. cohort (p. 462)
7. sensory (p. 465)
8. 1 (p. 465)
9. 15 (p. 466)
10. long (p. 465)
11. short (p. 465)
12. attention (p. 466)
13. short (p. 466)
14. 7 (p. 466)
15. episodic (p. 467)
16. semantic (p. 467)
17. encoding (p. 467)
18. pictures (p. 467)
19. recall (p. 468)
20. metamemory (p. 469)
21. fluid (p. 471)
22. crystallized (p. 471)
23. formal (p. 474)

MULTIPLE CHOICE

1. e (pp. 462-464)
2. d (p. 4640
3. d (p. 467)
4. b (p. 468)
5. b (p. 469)
6. e (p. 471)
7. c (p. 474)

MATCHING

1. a (p. 475)
2. b (p. 475)
3. b (p. 469)
4. a (p. 469)
5. b (p. 462)

CHAPTER SUMMARY

Chapter 19 concludes the section on <u>Early and middle adulthood</u> development by discussing social and emotional development in adulthood. Several theories of emotional and personal development are presented, and similarities and differences between these theories are highlighted.

The section on <u>Stages of adult emotional development</u> focuses on three major stages: entering adulthood, early adulthood, and middle adulthood. From the perspective of Erikson's psychosocial theory of development, the major developmental task of those <u>entering adulthood</u> is to resolve the tension between intimacy and isolation. In this stage adults learn how to commit themselves to relationships and find love. Unsuccessful resolution of this crisis leaves young adults in a state of psychological isolation. Research by Daniel Levinson on <u>early adulthood</u> among males, reveals several distinct stages or "seasons" of a man's life. The first stage is between the ages of 17 to 22, and the final stage is from age 80 on. Levinson suggested that a man's life forms a pattern of alternating periods of stability and flux. Between the ages of 40 and 45, Levinson suggests, a man enters a period of <u>midlife transition</u>. At this stage, he questions many of the beliefs and assumptions that have guided his life up to middle-age. Some men make radical changes in their living arrangements and styles during this period. For many men the midlife transition leads to a state of physical and psychological distress, or a midlife crisis. There is not complete consensus among researchers on the existence of a midlife crisis. <u>Middle adulthood</u> follows the midlife transition. This period is marked by emotional stability, as men feel more productive and satisfied than ever before, though some men may stagnate and enter a period of decline at this stage. Erikson characterized this period as one of crisis between generativity and self-absorption or stagnation. Generativity is caring about future generations, and self-absorption is self indulgent.

Results from Roger Gould's research on the development of both men and women were similar to Levinson's. These results help to validate Levinson's work, while simultaneously raising questions about whether the results are due to cohort effects. Gould offered a view of adulthood as a period of dynamic change and <u>transformations</u>. In this view adulthood unfolds in a fairly predictable sequence of changes in emotion, satisfaction, and motivation.

The section on <u>Sex differences in emotional development</u> summarizes research concerning the similarities and differences between men's and women's social and emotional development. Erik Erikson has asserted that the stages of psychosocial development are similar for men and women and, along with Levinson, he believes that males define themselves by growing independent in their relationships. Carol Gilligan offers a different view, suggesting that relationships form the core of girls' and women's lives. Gender seems to influence the ways that individuals relate to one another.

Personal relations are an important part of adult development and life satisfaction. By choosing a mate, people attempt to satisfy their needs for intimate connection with another person. The quality of intimate relationships varies greatly for different people. Not all intimate relationships are based on love. Relationships in marriage often involve complementary roles, in which one person is passive and the other assertive, or one nurturant and the other receptive, and so on. Research has shown three basic patterns to the power within marriages: (1) the husband is more powerful than the wife; (2) the husband acts as a senior partner, the wife as junior partner; and (3) the husband and wife are equal partners. Other studies have revealed more patterns than these basic three. Satisfaction with marriage seems to be based on intimacy and emotional security for women, and on loyalty and commitment to the future of the marriage for men. Other factors that affect individuals' satisfaction with their marriages include the degree of mutual admiration and respect between married individuals, the amount nurturance in women and self-confidence in men, and the degree of social maturity and achievement striving in both partners. Partners' satisfaction with their marriage influences how long the marriage lasts. External factors, such as career decisions and attraction to a person outside of the marriage, also influence whether marriage will end in divorce. Four out of ten marriages in the United States today end in divorce. Many people feel personal failure when their marriages end, but most remarry. Remarriage typically occurs within three years after a divorce, and the quality of the second marriage differs from the first.

The section on Other relationships indicates that adults have meaningful personal relationships with brothers and sister and friends. However, friendships tend to be more fragile than marriages and blood relations, and relationships between siblings tend to be less intense in adulthood than in childhood (especially among brothers).

The family can be viewed as a social system that is constantly changing or evolving through marriages, births, deaths, and divorces. Changes in one part of the family system tend to affect all other parts of the system. Being a parent today has different demands and qualities than several decades ago. Many women hold jobs today, and postpone having their first child until they are in their late twenties or thirties. Children have a strong influence on the marital satisfaction of parents, how well parents perform, how well parents perform as husband and

wife, how husband and wife evaluate each other, and the
sacrifices each makes for the sake of the family. The addition
of children in a family tends to shift the division of labor in
the household, with women tending to take on a greater number of
household and child care tasks. Parenthood is challenging and
satisfying at the same time. Many women feel that parenthood
enhances their sense of personal worth; many men feel that it
enhances their self-esteem. When the last child leaves home
parents face an empty nest. If the nest empties when it is
expected and prepared for, the transition is easier for family
members than when it empties abruptly, too early, or too late.
Most adults cope well with this normative life transition.
Unique life events, such as caring for frail parents, can
create an emotional and financial burden on the adult children
doing the caretaking. The accompanying stress of this situation
can destroy marriages, careers, and bank accounts.

The section on Work discusses the importance of work to the
development of a person's sense of self, the ways that people
choose work, and the process of career development. When young
adults are choosing work, they often do not understand the
everyday realities and requirements of occupations, or they do
not know what their own interests, skills, and qualities are for
seeking a suitable job. Unfortunately many people end up working
where they do by reason of accident, luck, sex, social class, and
proximity, rather than by reason of personal interests, skills,
and qualities. People who do develop along with their careers
follow a career path that intertwines their personal and work
identities. Some people follow an orderly career course over
many years. Beginning in adolescence, the orderly career path
starts with the crystallization stage, in which many fields are
explored for their match to personal interests, values, and
skills. During the specification stage, people find out more
about specific occupations, and their knowledge further
influences their career direction. By early adulthood, people
reach the implementation stage, in which they make an initial
commitment to an occupation. In their first five years of
working, people tend to change jobs more often than in later
years. Following some years of training and development within a
field, adults in their mid-twenties enter the stabilization
stage. In this stage they firm their positions within their
chosen field. A final stage before retirement is the
consolidation stage. This stage is usually reached by the mid-
thirties, and the worker advances as far as possible and
consolidates the gains he or she has made. Choice of occupations
as well as success in the occupation of choice is influenced by
an individual's personality and sex. Moreover, occupation may
affect personality characteristics. For example, the degree of
complexity of a job may affect self-esteem, anxiety,
responsiveness to change, moral standards, authoritarianism,
intellectual quality of leisure pursuits, and degree of
alienation.

ADULTHOOD

LEARNING OBJECTIVES

When you have finished studying Chapter 19 in both the text and this guide, you should be able to do the following:

1.   List the stages of adult emotional development.

2.   Discuss the major developmental task faced by young people entering adulthood as described by Erik Erikson.

3.   Describe the seasons of a man's life as defined by Daniel Levinson.

4.   Describe the contrasting perspectives of developmental psychologists on the topic of midlife transition and crisis.

5.   Discuss the major developmental crisis of middle adulthood from the perspective of Erik Erikson.

6.   Describe Roger Gould's theory of development during adulthood, and note any criticisms of his research.

7.   Contrast the views of Carol Gilligan with those of Erikson and Levinson on the issue of sex differences in emotional development.

8.   Summarize the age and sex differences in individuals' needs for emotional relationships.

9.   Briefly discuss the reasons and ways that people choose a mate.

10.   Describe the various patterns of relationships between married men and women.

11.   Discuss the factors that influence individuals' satisfaction with their marriages.

12.   Discuss the factors that influence individuals' decisions to divorce.

13.   Describe the quality of relationships between couples who remarry following their divorce.

14.   Describe the quality of relationships between adult siblings and adult friends.

15.   Describe how children affect the feelings and behaviors of their parents.

16. Describe how the family system changes following the birth of a child.

17. Discuss parents reactions to the departure of their last child from home.

18. Discuss how caring for frail parents affects the adult children doing the caretaking.

19. Discuss the role of work in adult social and emotional development.

20. Describe how young adults find a job.

21. Describe the various stages of career development for individuals who follow and orderly occupational course.

22. Describe the reciprocal relationship between personality and occupation.

KEY TERMS

Life structure (p. 481)

Midlife crisis (p. 484)

Equity theory (p. 490)

Autonomous mothers (p. 499)

Coupled mothers (p. 499)

Empty nest syndrome (p. 499)

Life cycle squeeze (p. 500)

ADULTHOOD

Crystallization stage (p. 502)

Specification stage (p. 502)

Implementation stage (p. 502)

Stabilization stage (p. 502)

Consolidation stage (p. 502)

STUDY QUESTIONS

1. What is the crisis between intimacy and isolation? What are the consequences for resolving or not resolving this crisis in early adulthood? (pp. 480-481)

2. According to Levinson, the seasons of a man's life form a life structure. Describe this structure and the various life transitions of men. (pp. 481-482)

3. Describe the method Levinson used to collect data for his theory of early adult development. How does Levinson's theory compare with Erikson's theory of development in early adulthood? (pp. 482-483)

4. What is the midlife transition? (pp. 483-484)

5. Developmental psychologists do not agree whether there is a midlife crisis. What is a midlife crisis and why is its existence suspect to some psychologists? (p. 484)

6. Describe Erikson's developmental crisis of generativity versus self-absorption. (pp. 484-485)

7. Compare and contrast Roger Gould's methods of study and theory of human development with Daniel Levinson's methods and theory. (pp. 485-486)

ADULTHOOD

8. Discuss the various views of developmental psychologist on the existence of differences in the emotional development of men and women. (pp. 486-489)

9. What are functions of personal relations for men and women of various ages? (p. 489)

10. How and why do individuals choose a mate? (pp. 489-490)

11. How do marriage partners divide power between them? (pp. 490-491)

12. What factors contribute to satisfaction with marriage and to decisions to end a marriage? (pp. 491-493)

13. How do remarriages differ from first marriages? Especially note any differences for men and women. (pp. 493-495)

14. How do sibling relations among adults differ from sibling relations among children? (p. 495)

15. Compare adult personal relationships with siblings with adult relationships with friends. (pp. 495-496)

16. Compare the friendships of women with those of men. (pp. 496-497)

17. How has the length of the cycle of family development changed in recent years? (p. 497)

18. How do children affect adults experience of parenthood? (pp. 497-498)

19. How do children change the division of labor in a family? (pp. 498-499)

20. How do changes in the division of labor within a marriage affect parents', especially mothers', feelings of satisfaction? (pp. 498-499)

21. What factors influence the satisfaction of autonomous mothers? Of coupled mothers? (p. 499)

22. What factors contribute to successful transition of parents facing the departure of their last child from the "nest"? (pp. 499-500)

23. Describe the life cycle squeeze. (p. 500)

24. What are the potential risks to adults who must care for their children and their frail parents simultaneously? (p. 500)

25. What is the role of work in an individual's personal development? (p. 501)

26. How do young people generally find jobs? (p. 501)

27. Describe the various stages of career development experienced by those people who follow an orderly occupational course. (p. 502)

ADULTHOOD

28. Describe the adolescent personalities of men and women who are successful at their careers in later adult life. (pp. 502-503)

29. Describe the personality differences between women who are committed to their careers with the those who are not committed. (p. 503)

30. How does a person's occupation or quality of work affect his or her personality? (pp. 503-504)

SELF-TEST, CHAPTER 19

COMPLETION QUESTIONS

1. The special developmental task of individuals entering adulthood is to resolve the tension between _intimacy_ and _isolation_.

2. Both Erikson and Daniel Levinson were influenced by _Freud)_ psychoanalytic theory.

3. According to Levinson, the midlife transition occurs in men between the ages of about _40_ and _45_.

4. _midlife_ crisis is a developmental state of physical and psychological distress that arises when developmental issues threaten to outstrip a person's resources for dealing with them.

5. According to Erikson, the developmental crisis of middle adulthood is between _generativ_ and _selfabsorption_.

6. Carol Gilligan suggests females locate their independence and identity _within_ their relationships with others.

7. Adult men subordinate their personal relationships to their aspirations and their _work_.

8. By choosing a mate, people try to satisfy their needs for _intimate_ connection with another person.

9. The _equity_ theory suggests that partners who offer many assets and few liabilities choose each other; those who offer few assets and many liabilities settle for each other.

10. During the first year of marriage, many partners assume _compmtry_ roles.

11. _4_ out of ten marriages in the United States today end in divorce.

12. Divorced people who remarry tend to do to within _3_ years.

13. When men remarry, they tend to look for women who are _young_ than they are, and women tend to look for _older_ men with good income.

14. Adult relationships with _siblings_ generally last longer than relationships with parents.

ADULTHOOD

15. Relationships with _friends_ are not bound by law or clear social customs, and they tend to be more fragile than relationships with family members.

16. On the average, adults _marry_ and have children later than adults did in the past.

17. Many modern women postpone having children until they are in their late _20_ or _30_ .

18. The _empty_ _nest_ syndrome supposedly affects parents when their last child leaves home.

19. When adult children must care for their frail parents as well as their own children, they may be caught in a _life_ _cycle_ squeeze.

20. In the _consolidation_ stage, people become experienced and knowledgeable in their job and advance as far as possible, until they retire.

MULTIPLE CHOICE

1. Young adults who remain psychosocially isolated, and experience shallow relationships with others, have not successfully resolved the crisis between:

   a. identity and role confusion
   b. generativity and self-absorption
   c. intimacy and isolation
   d. generativity and stagnation
   e. industry and inferiority

2. Levinson's descriptions of young men's transitions out of adolescence, and their grappling with the personality issue of autonomy, is similar to Erikson's descriptions of the tasks of:

   a. identity and intimacy
   b. intimacy and isolation
   c. identity and industry
   d. generativity and stagnation
   e. identity and role confusion

3.   Levinson found that 40-year-old men:

   a. are striving for direction
   b. evaluate their lives to this point, and are disappointed
      and disillusioned with their lives
   c. determine how to change the structure of their lives to
      meet the personal and social needs that confront them
   d. settle into a stable, fulfilling period
   e. none of the above

4.   Which of the following research findings is evidence
     AGAINST the existence of a midlife crisis?

   a. longitudinal data on Harvard graduates revealed that the
      frequency of divorce, of job changes, and of depression
      among middle-aged men was no higher than the frequency
      for these events throughout adulthood
   b. data on middle-class men and women born in the 1920s
      revealed that most men were satisfied with their work at
      midlife
   c. data on middle-class men and women born in the 1920s
      revealed that men and women felt self-confident,
      insightful, and resourceful in coping with stress at
      midlife
   d. none of the above
   e. a, b, and c

5.   According to Roger Gould, between the age of 35 and 43,
     people are in a period of:

   a. instability, turmoil, and psychological pain
   b. stability
   c. openness to new experiences
   d. satisfaction with family and career
   e. rebelliousness and anger

6.   Which of the following factors does NOT affect
     individuals' satisfaction with marriage?

   a. intimacy and emotional security
   b. loyalty
   c. mutual admiration
   d. opposing personalities
   e. mutual respect

ADULTHOOD

7. Which of the following statements is FALSE?

   a. children have little affect on the degree of satisfaction married people feel
   b. children affect how well parents perform as husband and wife
   c. married couples today have fewer children than couples in the 1960s
   d. children affect how parents evaluate one another as husband and wife
   e. most married couples today have children

8. Which of the following statements is TRUE?

   a. most young people will keep the same job throughout early and middle adulthood
   b. many young people obtain a job by chance rather than personal choice
   c. young adults today choose their jobs with adequate knowledge of the requirements of the occupation
   d. people who identify their personal interests, skills, and personal qualities are likely to find jobs that suit their interests, skills, and personal qualities
   e. only b and d

MATCHING

For each of the following statements indicate whether they are more likely to apply to male or to female adults, or both.

___a___ 1. feel the financial burden of caring for a frail parent
___c___ 2. find repetitive, fast-paced, mindless work to be alienating and injurious to health
___b___ 3. do more household chores and child care tasks after the birth of the first child
___b___ 4. have a very close relationship with an adult brother
___c___ 5. remarry within 3 years of a divorce
___a___ 6. to feel happy in a marriage
___a___ 7. wield power directly in a marriage
___b___ 8. to be nurturant and supportive of a spouse
___c___ 9. need to resolve the tension between intimacy and isolation upon entering adulthood
___c___ 10. experience many changes in emotions and motivation, and relations with others throughout adulthood

a. more likely to apply to male adults
b. more likely to apply to female adults
c. likely to apply equally to male and female adults

ANSWERS TO THE SELF-TEST, CHAPTER 19

COMPLETION QUESTIONS

1. intimacy, isolation (p. 480)
2. Freud's (p. 481)
3. 40, 45 (p. 483)
4. Midlife (p. 484)
5. generativity, self-absorption (p. 485)
6. within (p. 488)
7. work (p. 488)
8. intimate (p. 489)
9. equity (p. 490)
10. complementary (p. 490)
11. Four (p. 493)
12. 3 (p. 493)
13. younger, older (p. 494)
14. sibling (p. 495)
15. friends (p. 495)
16. marry (p. 497)
17. 20s, 30s (p. 497)
18. empty nest (p. 499)
19. life cycle (p. 500)
20. consolidation (p. 502)

MULTIPLE CHOICE

1. c (p. 480)
2. a (p. 482)
3. b (p. 483)
4. e (p. 484)
5. a (p. 485)
6. d (p. 491)
7. a (p. 497)
8. e (p. 501)

MATCHING

1. a (p. 500)
2. c (p. 504)
3. b (p. 498)
4. b (p. 495)
5. a (p. 493)
6. a (p. 492)
7. a (p. 491)
8. b (p. 490)
9. c (p. 480)
10. c (p. 480)

CHAPTER SUMMARY

Chapter 20 outlines physical development in late adulthood.
Theories of aging are discussed, and physical changes in the body
are described. Disease trends concomitant with aging are noted,
and the role of habits in health maintenance is reviewed.

The section Biological perspectives on aging explains several
theories of aging. Factors that determine the biological limits
on the human lifespan, and what makes people age are two
fundamental questions researchers ask. Programmed theories of
aging suggest that DNA controls the aging process, and that
individuals go through a succession of predictable biological
events, including the aging of cells and organs. Studies of
individuals who age prematurely or who age abnormally suggest
that aging is governed by the actions of many different genes.
Laboratory research has shown that human cells have limited
lifespans, termed the Hayflick limit. However, the Hayflick
limit is not consistently replicated in natural environments.
The fact that each species has a different maximum lifespan,
identical twins have similar lifespans, and longevity of parents
and grandparents predicts the probability of a child's longevity,
are additional pieces of evidence for a programmed theory of
aging. Investigations of programmed deterioration suggest that
(1) certain genes that trigger gradual aging and death are
activated at particular points in the lifespan, (2) young genes
are turned off by aging genes during middle age, or (3) youthful
genes somehow change in middle age. Estrogen has been implicated
as a hormone that protects women from aging prior to menopause.
The hypothalamus and the immune system are also being studied
for their roles in programmed aging. A second class of theories,
wear and tear theories, propose that functional damage sustained
throughout life is responsible for aging. Bodies repair
themselves less effectively with each incident of physical
damage. DNA repair theory focuses on long-term damage to DNA
resulting from exposure to ultraviolet light as well as other
sources. This theory suggests that the rate of repair always
lags behind the rate of damage. Accumulation of damage affects
the functioning of nerve and muscle cells. Cross-linkage theory
proposes that living cells age as a result of cross-links that
form between cells. These cross links are formed during cell
metabolism, and as they increase in number tissue loses its
suppleness. The free radical theory proposes that inherently
unstable chemicals bond easily with other chemicals, and this
bonding can damage cell membranes and chromosomes. Lipofuscins,
inert brown pigments that accumulate in many body cells, are also
implicated in aging. These lipofuscins increase in the cell of
an aging body and interfere with functioning. Presently no one
theory of aging explains all the questions researchers have about
the aging process.

LATE ADULTHOOD

Physical changes associated with aging are usually gradual.
Illness is not an inevitable part of being old; most people do
not have major health problems until they pass the age of 75.
Skin may grow paler with age as cells containing pigment
decrease. Additionally, environmental exposure, particularly to
the sun, ages the skin. Sunlight interferes with DNA production
and protein synthesis, can lead to thin and wrinkled skin, or to
skin cancer. The skeletal, cardiovascular, respiratory,
gastrointestinal, excretory, reproductive and nervous systems all
lose efficiency with age. There is debate over whether these
changes result from normal or from secondary aging, caused by
lifestyle and environmental exposure. Changes in the skeletal
system include thinner bones and shrinking spines. Currently it
is estimated that men shrink one inch and women two inches as
their posture changes. After age 30, bones begin to lose their
calcium, particularly those of women. Bones can still repair
fractures, though not as quickly as before. Osteoporosis, a
condition of pitted and brittle bones, occurs four times more
often in post menopausal women than in men, and is a major
contributor to broken bones in older persons. Possible causes of
osteoporosis include lower levels of estrogen, inactivity,
lactase deficiency, and dietary factors such as low-calcium or
high amounts of animal protein. Osteoarthritis, a painful
degeneration of the joints, results from wear and tear on the
skeletal system. Heredity, hormones, and diet contribute to this
disorder which is common and severe in persons up to 80 years
old. Past the age of 17, few people get tooth decay in their
sound teeth, however, periodontal disease is increasingly common
with age and results in lost teeth. Normal aging of the
cardiovascular system results in a brownish-looking heart covered
with fat. Additionally, the aging heart is larger, beats less
quickly, and the proportion of muscle to collagen drops.
Arteries stiffen with age and become less efficient at
transporting blood. A more rigid rib cage and less elastic
muscles contribute to shallow breathing, a sign of a less
efficient respiratory system. Changes inside and outside of the
lungs contribute to decreased breathing efficiency. Signs of a
less efficient gastrointestinal system include weakened muscles
that move food through the body, diminished production of
hydrochloric acid in the stomach, and fewer enzymes secreted in
the intestines. The liver and gallbladder continue to function
well in most people, although the ability of the liver to
metabolize certain drugs diminishes. The bladder and kidneys,
parts of the excretory system, shrink with age, but still work
fairly efficiently for most people. With respect to the
reproductive system, sexuality can continue throughout life, even
though sexual response slows with age. Human sexual activity is
largely independent of reproduction, but is related to declines
in sex hormones, as well as to social factors. The brain, part
of the nervous system, loses weight, shrinks, and its interior
ventricles enlarge with age. Neurons, dendrites, and axons in
certain regions of the brain die, lipofuscin builds up, and some

unconditioned reflexes disappear. Sleep becomes shorter, lighter, and more restless. With age, neurotransmitters weaken or are metabolized differently as neurons die. These changes weaken some autonomic functions, but overall have little effect on functioning.

The section Disease and aging discusses acute illness and injuries, chronic illness, and health and expectations. Acute illnesses in old age are fewer than in younger years, but are more severe and are likely to be complicated by certain aspects of normal aging. Chronic illnesses such as diabetes, arthritis, emphysema, and heart disease are very common among older people. Health and expectations highlights the importance of taking people's expectations into account when evaluating their level of conditioning.

Finally, Habits and health describes the role of smoking, diet, and exercise in the development and ascerbation of disease. Improvements in health habits are likely to translate into significant gains in longevity and quality of life for aging Americans.

LEARNING OBJECTIVES

When you have finished studying Chapter 20 in both the text and this guide, you should be able to do the following:

1. Describe the basic premises of programmed theories of aging.

2. Discuss research supporting programmed theories of aging.

3. Explain the wear and tear theories of aging.

4. Describe changes in the skin that occur from normal and secondary aging.

5. Describe changes in the skeletal system as a result of aging.

6. Describe cardiovascular system changes, particularly in the arteries, resulting from age.

7. Note how and why the respiratory system loses efficiency over time.

8. Explain changes in the gastrointestinal system.

9. Describe factors affecting sexuality and sexual response in late adulthood.

10. List changes in the autonomic and central nervous systems, in neurons and in neuroglia that occur with age.

11. Explain how the severity and frequency of acute illnesses differs between childhood and late adulthood.

12. Cite common chronic illnesses older adults experience.

13. Discuss the role of expectations in evaluating health.

14. Explain how smoking affects health.

15. Discuss the role of diet in health maintenance and illness prevention.

16. Describe the benefits of exercise for the elderly.

KEY TERMS

Programmed theories (p. 510)

Progeria (p. 511)

Werner's syndrome (p. 511)

Alzheimer's disease (p. 511)

Hayflick limit (p. 511)

Wear-and-tear theories (p. 513)

DNA repair theory (p. 513)

Cross-linkage theory (p. 513)

Free radical theory (p. 513)

Melanocytes (p. 514)

Melanin (p. 515)

Osteoporosis (p. 515)

Osteoarthritis (p. 516)

Elastin (p. 517)

Alveoli (p. 518)

Astrocytes (p. 526)

Acute illness (p. 529)

Chronic illness (p. 530)

STUDY QUESTIONS

1.   Construct an argument for a programmed theory of aging,
     using evidence discussed in the text.   (pp. 510-513)

LATE ADULTHOOD

2. Compare the various wear-and-tear theories of aging.
    What are the major differences between these theories and
    programmed theories of aging? (pp. 513-514)

3. Many bodily changes result from normal aging, while others
    occur as a result of lifestyle and environmental exposure.
    For the following parts of the body note what major changes
    occur, and whether these changes are thought to result from
    normal aging, lifestyle and environmental factors, or both.

    (a) Skin (pp. 514-515)

    (b) Skeletal system (pp. 515-517)

    (c) Cardiovascular system (pp. 517-518)

    (d) Respiratory system   (pp. 518-519)

(e) Gastrointestinal system (pp. 519-520)

4. Describe how sexuality is expressed in late adulthood, and note factors affecting the expression of sexuality. (pp. 521-522)

5. Discuss changes in the nervous system that come with age, and how these changed affect functioning. (pp. 522-528)

6. Describe the chronic illnesses most older adults will experience. What risk factors are associated with these illnesses? (pp. 529-531)

7. Explain how health habits (smoking, diet, and exercise) can increase risk of illness, or act as a protective mechanism against illness. (pp. 533-539)

SELF-TEST, CHAPTER 20

COMPLETION QUESTIONS

1. Theories that suggest aging is under the direction of the DNA in human genes are called _____ theories of aging.

2. People with _____ syndrome show signs of abnormal aging in their teens or twenties.

3. _____ is a rare disease that, beginning in infancy, turns young children into aged old men and women.

4. The scientist Leonard _____ discovered that the individual human cell has a limited lifespan.

5. Pronounced pitted and brittle bones are signs of a condition called _____.

6. Past the age of _____, few people get tooth decay in their sound teeth.

7. Illnesses that last for a long time, resist cure, and tend to worsen over time are called _____ illnesses.

8. One major risk factor for cardiovascular disease is high blood pressure, also called _____.

9. Diets low in _____ and high in natural _____ are likely to prevent obesity.

10. One technique for studying brain activity, the _____, picks up electrical impulses between nerve cells and charts them.

MULTIPLE CHOICE

1. The discovery of the Hayflick limit lent support for which theory of aging?

   a. DNA repair theory
   b. programmed theory
   c. cross-linkage theory
   d. free radical theory
   e. lipofuscin theory

2.   Exposure to sunlight

   a. reduces the skin's ability to produce melanin
   b. affects dark-complected people more than
      light-complected people
   c. may cause skin cancer for light-complected people
   d. can cause a Vitamin A deficiency
   e. none of the above

3.   With respect to the skeletal system, with age

   a. men shrink about 2 inches and women shrink about 1 inch
   b. women lose about half of the density in their bones
   c. skeletal bones are no longer able to repair fractures
   d. osteoporosis causes bone breakage more easily than normal
   e. all of the above

4.   Osteoporosis

   a. is found twice as often in post menopausal women than in
      men
   b. is a major factor in bone fractures
   c. may be caused by high levels of estrogen
   d. is affected by a lack of animal protein
   e. all of the above

5.   With age, the heart

   a. changes color from brown to red
   b. loses much of its muscle tone
   c. gets smaller in size
   d. beats more quickly
   e. all of the above

6.   Older people breathe more shallowly than younger people
     because

   a. their rib cages are more rigid
   b. the muscles that move the chest while breathing are more
      elastic
   c. lungs are blackened by carbon particles
   d. the alveoli grow in size
   e. oxygen in the alveoli decreases

7. The gastrointestinal system is less efficient in older people because

    a. muscular contractions that move food along the digestive tract are not as effective
    b. the stomach's secretion of hydrochloric acid increases, especially in men
    c. the amount of enzymes secreted in the intestines increases, causing ulcers
    d. the smooth muscle in the wall of the large intestine becomes enlarged due to engorged blood vessels
    e. the liver doubles in size

8. Kidneys

    a. are one of the first bodily systems to be negatively affected in the aging process
    b. begin to shrink after about age 50
    c. work fairly efficiently for most older people
    d. are more likely to be ineffective in women than in men
    e. are responsible for most cases of hypertension

9. Sexual responsiveness in older women is NOT influenced by which of the following?

    a. presence of a stable partner
    b. social class
    c. health
    d. attitudes toward sexuality
    e. race

10. As people age, the autonomic nervous system

    a. undergoes marked deterioration
    b. is affected by the development of new neurotransmitters
    c. shows only slight slowing of some internal organ functions
    d. a and b only
    e. b and c only

11. Sleep in older persons is affected by

    a. reduced bladder capacity
    b. sleep apnea
    c. level of physical fitness
    d. medication
    e. all of the above

12. Astrocytes

    a. are star-shaped connective tissue between neurons in the
       brain and neurons in the outer limbs
    b. increase as neurons or dendrites increase
    c. directly affect speech areas of the brain
    d. prevent neurotransmitters from building up between nerve
       cells
    e. are discovered using an EBG test

13. Acute illnesses

    a. are more common in older adults than in children
    b. are more severe in older adults than in children
    c. are fairly easy to diagnose in older adults because they
       are so common
    d. a and b only
    e. all of the above

14. Cardiovascular disease

    a. is a chronic illness
    b. is the leading cause of death for American men and women
    c. is affected by both inherited and environmental factors
    d. a and c only
    e. all of the above

15. Older people's ratings of their health

    a. are quite accurate
    b. rarely agree with doctors' ratings of their health
    c. are not good predictors of future health and illness
    d. are influenced by their children's evaluations of their
       health
    e. b and c

16. Which of the following statements concerning health habits
    is FALSE?

    a. smoking is a large contributor to chronic illness
    b. stopping smoking late in life will not have much of an
       effect because the damage has already been done
    c. living alone is associated with poor dietary practices
    d. elevated cholesterol is a large contributor to
       cardiovascular disease
    e. women become sedentary before men

LATE ADULTHOOD

MATCHING

Using the letters below, indicate whether each physical development is a result of normal aging, of secondary aging, or of a combination of the two.

_____ 1. paler skin
_____ 2. thin and wrinkled skin
_____ 3. spine shrinkage
_____ 4. osteoarthritis
_____ 5. changes in the walls of arteries
_____ 6. decreased breathing efficiency
_____ 7. development of gallstones
_____ 8. hypertension

a. result of normal aging
b. result of secondary aging
c. result of both normal and secondary aging

ANSWERS TO THE SELF-TEST, CHAPTER 20

COMPLETION QUESTIONS

1. programmed (p. 519)
2. Werner's (p. 511)
3. Progeria (p. 511)
4. Hayflick (p. 511)
5. osteoporosis (p. 515)
6. 17 (p. 516)
7. chronic (p. 530)
8. hypertension (p. 531)
9. fat; fiber (p. 534)
10. electroencephalogram (EEG)(p. 526)

MULTIPLE CHOICE

1. b (pp. 510-514)
2. e (pp. 514-515)
3. d (p. 515)
4. b (pp. 515-516)
5. b (p. 517)
6. a (p. 518)
7. a (pp. 519-520)
8. c (p. 520)
9. e (pp. 521-522)
10. c (pp. 522-523)
11. e (p. 524)
12. d (pp. 525-527)
13. b (p. 529)
14. e (pp. 530-531)
15. a (pp. 531-532)
16. b (p. 534)

MATCHING

1. a (p. 514)
2. c (p. 515)
3. c (p. 515)
4. c (p. 516)
5. c (p. 517)
6. c (p. 518)
7. c (p. 520)
8. b (p. 531)

CHAPTER SUMMARY

Chapter 21, <u>Cognitive development</u>, differentiates between what are considered normal declines in cognition and declines considered to be pathological. Areas of possible cognitive growth are also addressed.

<u>Normal declines in cognition</u> include decrements in information processing, intellectual abilities, psychomotor performance, and reasoning and problem solving. Unless these declines are associated with disease they are slight and affect only some individuals. Cross-sectional research indicates that <u>information processing skills</u> such as learning, thinking, and remembering become less efficient in late adulthood. However, older people adapt to changes in their cognitive functioning. Beginning in their sixties, older adults take longer to be classically conditioned than younger adults. Operant conditioning can succeed with older adults, even among those with organic brain disease. Although vocabulary remains the same, performance on verbal learning tasks and encoding ability appears to decline with time, possibly a result of slowing perceptual processes. Although the overall results are mixed, some older adults have been successfully taught cognitive skills such as inductive reasoning, hypothesis testing strategies, and perspective taking. Observed age differences in learning may be influenced by the pacing of the task, and by the motivation, caution, and distractibility of the subject, making it difficult to determine whether declines are a result of aging. Laboratory experiments run at a quick pace may underestimate the abilities of older persons, as might anxiety produced in testing situations. The tendency for older persons to be more cautious and less able to focus on a learning task, plus interference from previously learned materials, also may underestimate ability. Declines in <u>intellectual abilities</u> such as fluid intelligence may result from less attention to incidental features of the environment. Research on changes in IQ scores has produced mixed results, with cross-sectional research showing declines in IQ from early adulthood on and longitudinal research showing increases in scores until age 60. Today researchers believe cohort effects (differences in education) are responsible for large cross-sectional differences, and that there are small declines in intelligence among people in their fifties and older. <u>Terminal drop</u> is a term for marked declines in IQ shortly prior to death. <u>Psychomotor performance</u> declines with age, but older people adapt to changes in their sensory functioning. Finally, older adults do quite well at <u>reasoning and problem solving</u> concerning everyday problems, but do more poorly than younger adults on Piagetian-type tasks, such as tests of formal operations.

<u>Pathological declines in cognition</u> include acute and chronic brain dysfunction. Impaired memory, intellect, judgment and

concentration, and exaggerated or shallow emotions, are all symptoms of organic brain disorders. People who suffer from <u>acute brain dysfunction</u> may be confused, in a stupor, have fluctuating levels of awareness, or be delirious, but these symptoms are reversible. Ten to 20 percent suffer from delirium, a disorder that disturbs brain metabolism. Possible causes of acute brain dysfunction include medicine, malnutrition, brain tumors, liver and cardiovascular disease, stroke, fever, emphysema and acute alcoholism. When diagnosed correctly, acute brain dysfunction lasts less than one week; without treatment, people may develop chronic brain disorder and die, which many do. <u>Chronic brain dysfunction</u> severely impairs the cognitive functioning of about five percent of those over 65, and mildly to moderately impairs another 10 percent. Half of all older adults with chronic brain dysfunction have Alzheimer's disease, which causes severe cognitive disability. More common in women than in men, Alzheimer's has a hereditary component and afflicts both middle aged and older adults. It is incurable, has a slow onset, and its symptoms frequently are misinterpreted. Multi-infarct dementia accounts for 20 percent of chronic brain dysfunction, and results from having the blood supply to the brain cut off. It is more common among men and also may be misdiagnosed. Parkinson's disease, found primarily among adults over 60, also affects more men than women. Tremors associated with Parkinson's affect the functioning of fingers, arms, eyelids, and tongue; facial expression of emotion is also impaired. Dopamine deficiencies are characteristic of persons with Parkinson's disease.

Growing old is not necessarily negative. Creativity and wisdom are areas of <u>possible growth in cognition</u>. Some individuals remain very <u>creative</u> into old age, especially those who continue to exercise their creative skills. <u>Wisdom</u>, which includes a mixture of intellect, feeling, and intuition, is not a trait of all older adults, but does take time to develop and therefore may flourish in old age.

LEARNING OBJECTIVES

When you have finished studying Chapter 21 in both the text and this guide, you should be able to do the following:

1. Describe the normal declines in information processing skills that occur with age.

2. Discuss factors that influence age differences in learning.

3. Explain the results of cross-sectional and longitudinal research on intelligence, and note the current scientific thinking on IQ and age.

4.   Explain terminal drop and its possible causes.

5.   Describe changes in reasoning and problem solving related
     to age.

6.   Distinguish between acute and chronic brain dysfunction,
     their symptoms, causes, and treatments.

7.   Describe the various types of chronic brain dysfunction
     discussed in the text.

8.   Note possible areas of growth in old age.

KEY TERMS

Terminal drop (p. 551)

Organic brain disorders (p. 555)

Acute brain dysfunction (p. 556)

Chronic brain dysfunction (p. 556)

Delirium (p. 556)

Multi-infarct dementia (p. 559)

Parkinson's disease (p. 559)

LATE ADULTHOOD

STUDY QUESTIONS

1. Describe age changes in classical and operant conditioning, explaining why it might be harder to condition older people. (pp. 544-545)

2. How does verbal learning change with age? What factors might explain these changes? (pp. 545-546)

3. Describe how pacing, motivation, caution and distractibility might underestimate the skills of an older individual. (pp. 546-548)

4. Does IQ decline with age? Defend your response with research evidence. (pp. 548-551)

5. What factors might explain the phenomenon terminal drop? (pp. 551-552)

6. How well do older persons adapt to changes in their environment? Cite ways in which older adults adapt to these changes. (p. 552)

7. Describe changes in reasoning and problem solving older adults experience. How relevant are these changes to living in the "real world"? (pp. 552-555)

8. Cite symptoms of organic brain disorder. (p. 555)

9. Compare and contrast acute and chronic brain dysfunction in terms of the symptoms, causes and treatment. (pp. 556-560)

10. What does the research say concerning creativity in later life? (pp. 560-561)

11. How is wisdom perceived in America? How does age relate to wisdom? (pp. 561-564)

LATE ADULTHOOD

SELF-TEST, CHAPTER 21

COMPLETION QUESTIONS

1. When previously learned material interferes with the learning of new material the phenomenon is called _proactive_ interference.

2. The ability to manipulate abstract symbols is called _fluid_ intelligence.

3. _Terminal drop_ describes marked declines in IQ shortly before death.

4. People with organic brain disorders whose symptoms are reversible are said to suffer from _acute_ brain dysfunction; those with irreversible symptoms have _chronic_ brain dysfunction.

5. About _half_ percent of the older adults with chronic brain dysfunction suffer from Alzheimer's disease.

6. When blood clots repeatedly cut off blood to the brain, a person is diagnosed as having _multi_ - _infarct_ dementia.

7. Parkinson's disease is characterized by a deficiency of the neurotransmitter _dopamine_

8. In western cultures, wisdom is considered a mixture of intellect, feeling, and _intuition_.

9. It has been suggested that some older adults may be so highly motivated to perform well on learning experiments that their level of _anxiety_ increases, causing them to perform more poorly.

MULTIPLE CHOICE

1. It may be harder to succeed at operant conditioning with older adults because

   a. changes in the central nervous system may have weakened involuntary responses
   b. declines in sensory acuteness have occurred making stimuli feel less unpleasant
   c. older adults take longer to register and respond to stimuli
   d. rewards that are effective with younger adults are less effective with older adults
   e. all of the above

2.   Verbal learning

a. appears to decline after age 40
b. is influenced by diminished decoding ability
c. may result from quickened perceptual processes
d. is affected by how fast the task is paced
e. all of the above

3.   Which of the following statements regarding declines in
fluid intelligence in older adults is NOT TRUE?

a. declines may result from paying less attention to
incidental features of the environment
b. declines may result from problems in organizing
information
c. declines may result from problems in focusing attention
d. declines may result from expectations individuals have
about a task
e. declines appear to be fairly permanent

4.   IQ test scores

a. begin to fall in a person's twenties, according to
longitudinal research
b. drop markedly after age 50
c. increase until age 30, then decline, according to
longitudinal studies
d. are affected by exposure to radio, TV, and sophisticated
technology
e. peak at successively earlier ages, beginning in 1916

5.   Laboratory tests of formal operations

a. are often poor indicators of real world functioning
b. indicate that older adults do as well as younger adults
c. are not related to scores on IQ tests
d. indicate that older men perform much better than older
women
e. do not seem to be affected by training programs

6.   Acute brain dysfunction

a. affects a majority of older adults
b. has a good prognosis if diagnosed properly
c. has symptoms significantly different from those of
chronic brain dysfunction
d. affects women more frequently than men
e. all of the above

7.   Chronic brain dysfunction

   a. severely impairs the cognitive functioning of about 25%
      of those over 65
   b. usually develops among those in their 50's and 60's
   c. is reversible
   d. may have some genetic components
   e. all of the above

8.   Alzheimer's disease

   a. is only curable in about 1% of all cases
   b. is more common among men than women
   c. is associated with lack of the neurotransmitter dopamine
   d. has a genetic component
   e. all of the above

MATCHING

A. Match each statement to the corresponding letters below.

_d_ 1. suggested wisdom comes as the conflict between despair over impending death and integrity over a meaningful life is resolved

_f_ 2. suggested that wisdom only develops when people have lived a long time according to advanced moral principles

_a_ 3. suggested creativity is possible only if important conflicts from the past are resolved

_g_ 4. indicated that older individuals are no wiser than persons of other ages

_c_ 5. in this culture, wisdom is considered a mixture of intellect, feeling, and intuition

a. Birren   f. Kohlberg
b. college students   g. older adults
c. eastern   h. Piaget
d. Erikson   i. Skinner
e. Freud   j. western

B. Use the letters below to indicate whether each statement is associated with acute brain dysfunction, chronic brain dysfunction, or both.

_a_ 1. reversible symptoms
_a_ 2. delirium
_c_ 3. impaired judgment
_b_ 4. genetic component
_b_ 5. multi-infarct dementia
_b_ 6. problems with neurotransmitters
_c_ 7. impaired memory

a. acute brain dysfunction
b. chronic brain dysfunction
c. both acute and chronic brain dysfunction

ANSWERS TO THE SELF-TEST, CHAPTER 21

COMPLETION QUESTIONS

1. proactive (p. 548)
2. fluid (p. 548)
3. terminal drop (p. 551)
4. acute; chronic (p. 556)
5. half (p. 557)
6. multi-infarct (p. 559)
7. dopamine (p. 559)
8. intuition (p. 561)
9. arousal or anxiety (p. 547)

MULTIPLE CHOICE

1. d (pp. 544-545)
2. d (pp. 545-546)
3. e (pp. 548-549)
4. d (pp. 549-550)
5. a (pp. 553-554)
6. b (pp. 556-557)
7. d (pp. 557-559)
8. d (pp. 557-559)

MATCHING

A.

1. d (p. 562)
2. f (p. 562)
3. a (p. 561)
4. g (p. 562)
5. j (p. 561)

B.

1. a (p. 556)
2. a (p. 556)
3. c (p. 555)
4. b (p. 558)
5. b (p. 559)
6. b (p. 558)
7. c (p. 555)

CHAPTER SUMMARY

Chapter 22, <u>Social development</u>, discusses personality and emotional development, family and personal relationships, work and leisure, and community involvement in late adulthood.

<u>Personality and emotional development</u> in late adulthood is a hotly debated research area. Evidence presented in the section <u>Stability and change in personality</u> indicates, however, that self-concept, and therefore personality, is stable during adulthood. When personalities do change it is generally in response to life events or crises. One personality trait, introversion, has been found to increase in adulthood. Data also suggest that feelings of life satisfaction are stable over time. Health, activity level, money, social class, social interactions, marital status, and personality traits all influence ratings of satisfaction with life. For city residents, happiness with housing arrangements is the most significant factor in life satisfaction; for rural dwellers, health is the key factor. Not much has been written concerning <u>Emotional development in late adulthood</u>. Erikson theorized that adults who successfully resolve the conflict between feelings of integrity and despair emerge with a sense of wisdom.

<u>Family and personal relationships</u> in late adulthood may be both painful, such as widowhood, and rewarding, such as enjoying spouses, children, grandchildren, siblings, and friends. Marital satisfaction is high in late adulthood, and is positively affected by an active sexual relationship and egalitarian and cooperative interactions. More women than men experience <u>widowhood</u>. When a spouse is lost between the ages of 50 and 70, more men than women remarry. Many factors affect adjustment to widowhood, including earlier dependence on the spouse who died; the couple's earlier involvement in family, community and work; social and economic resources; and the perception that the widowhood was "on time". Relations with <u>brothers, sisters, and friends</u> may deepen in late adulthood, especially among adults who have never married or who are widowed. As people age, siblings may become substitute parents or spouses. Social class, sex, and employment status all affect friendships. Older adults who are married see more of their friends than do unmarried adults. <u>Grandparents</u> today may be middle aged or older adults, and 40 percent of older adults are great grandparents. Although many grandparents say they take pleasure from their grandchildren, few state that feelings of satisfaction with their lives derive from their involvement with their grandchildren. Satisfaction with the grandparent role is influenced by age and by gender roles. Styles of relating to grandchildren vary, and include formal, fun-seeking, and distant. Some grandmothers assume the role of surrogate parent, tending children as mothers work. Most grandchildren are close to their grandparents until they are about 10 years old. Although in

this country each generation within a family usually prefers to live in its own household, relations among generations are close and frequent enough to make the American family a modified extended family. Many older adults see their children often, and married daughters are more likely than married sons to have contact with their elderly parents. Most elderly parents and their middle-aged children say that they feel close to each other, and older adults value their children's respect and affection. Elderly parents and their children try to influence each other.

The section Work and leisure covers retirement, leisure, and education. Legally, individuals cannot be made to retire before age 70, though many choose to retire at age 62 and accept lowered benefits. Attitudes toward paid retirement have changed over the years. Previously it was believed that retirement pay was for disabled workers only; now people see retirement as a reward. For most, income drops substantially with retirement, and older women are less well off than are older men. Three fourths of retirees say they want work. Retirement occurs in part because of age discrimination: older adults are believed to be less competent in the workplace. Stereotypes of older adults are reinforced by hiring and firing trends, though evidence suggests that older workers are no worse, and in some cases better, than their younger counterparts in certain aspects of the job. Research on adjustment to retirement has produced mixed results, with effects being positive, negative, or neutral depending on the individual's circumstances. Personality traits, attitudes, marital status, and finances all affect adjustment to retirement. Leisure time increases with retirement, and the activities people find most pleasurable change over the course of the lifespan. Goals of any leisure activity include relaxation, diversion, and developmental, creative, and sensual pleasures. People choose leisure activities that complement their roles and values, and the satisfaction of retired persons is strongly related to their level of social involvement. Many older adults engage in formal Education to fill leisure time, grow personally, or improve their functioning in society. Older adults do as well or better than younger adults in educational endeavors.

Community involvement by the elderly includes religious, political, legal, and economic activities. Religious involvement correlates highly with satisfaction about one's life. Throughout adulthood more people participate in religious activities than all other voluntary community activities combined. There is some indication that religion becomes more meaningful as adults age. Older adults are politically active, and tend to vote for their own self-interest. They are also less conservative than presumed, and don't become more conservative over time. Personality characteristics evident in adolescence influence political outlooks later in life. Finally, legal and economic issues discusses ways that laws may reinforce negative stereotypes about the elderly. The elderly spend more than younger adults on housing and medical care, and less on clothes, furniture, transportation, personal care and leisure.

LEARNING OBJECTIVES

When you have finished studying Chapter 22 in both the text and this guide, you should be able to do the following:

1. Describe changes in the personality in late adulthood.

2. List factors affecting personality changes in late adulthood.

3. Discuss correlates of life satisfaction among the elderly.

4. Describe emotional development in late adulthood.

5. Discuss influences on satisfaction with marriage among older adults.

6. Note factors affecting adjustment to widowhood.

7. Describe the relationships elderly persons have with siblings and friends.

8. Describe the various roles grandparents may assume.

9. Discuss the importance of grandchildren to grandparent's satisfaction with life.

10. Discuss intergenerational relationships.

11. List factors influencing satisfaction with retirement.

12. Describe ways in which older persons are discriminated against.

13. Describe how individuals adjust to retirement.

14. List the functions of leisure, and note the type of leisure activities the elderly participate in.

15. Describe how formal education fits into the lifestyle of the elderly individual.

16. Discuss the role of religion in the lives of older adults.

17. Describe the political involvement of older adults.

18. Discuss legal and economic issues facing the elderly.

LATE ADULTHOOD

KEY TERMS

Normative stability (p. 568)

Modified extended family (p. 577)

STUDY QUESTIONS

1. How stable is the personality in adulthood? Discuss factors affecting personality changes, if any, during this period. (pp. 568-570)

2. What factors predict how satisfied the elderly are with their lives? (pp. 571-572)

3. Describe factors affecting adjustment to widowhood. Why do men appear to have more difficulty coping with the loss of a spouse? (pp. 573-574)

4. Discuss the different ways grandparents relate to their grandchildren. (pp. 575-577)

5. Describe the relationship between most older adults and their middle-aged children. (pp. 577-578)

6. Discuss adjustment to retirement, and factors which influence satisfaction with it. (pp. 578-581)

7. Describe the functions of leisure, and factors affecting leisure activity among the elderly. (pp. 581-582)

8. Describe the educational opportunities currently available to older adults. (pp. 582-583)

9. How important is religious involvement to older adults? Does level of religious involvement change with age? (p. 584)

10. Describe the political activity of older adults, and factors predictive of political involvement in older individuals. (pp. 584-585)

LATE ADULTHOOD

SELF-TEST, CHAPTER 22

COMPLETION QUESTIONS

1. For older adults living in rural areas, _____ is the most important factor in their feelings of well-being and satisfaction; for older adults in cities, _____ is the most significant factor.

2. Older married adults are _____ satisfied with their marriages than are middle-aged couples.

3. Erikson suggests that older adults need to resolve the conflict between feelings of _____ and _____.

4. There are over _____ times as many widows as widowers in America.

5. Today about _____ percent of older adults are great grandparents.

6. Even though most generations of American families live apart, individuals have enough close and frequent contact to describe their relationship as a _____ _____ family.

7. The law today provides that no one can be forced to retire before age _____.

8. Whether retired people are generally satisfied with their lives or not is best predicted by their level of _____ _____.

9. Among older adults, factors such as health and _____ interfere with religious participation away from home.

10. Older adults vote _____ than people from other age groups.

MULTIPLE CHOICE

1. Studies of normative stability show that:

    a. personality changes dramatically from young to late adulthood
    b. personality is stable during adulthood
    c. personalities may change, but generally in response to life events or life crises
    d. stereotypes of the elderly are often supported by research evidence
    e. b and c only

2. The Costa and McCrae study of how personality dimensions change over time found that:

a. high levels of neuroticism were associated with health complaints and dissatisfaction with life
b. neuroticism and extraversion-introversion were quite stable over a 10-year period, but openness changed quite a bit
c. men who were very open tended to score high on measures of religious and economic values
d. men high in extraversion were more likely to work as psychologists, psychiatrists and ministers than as bankers, veterinarians or undertakers.
e. men high in introversion got themselves involved in lawsuits often

3. Older adults who report a greater than average satisfaction with their marriages are likely to

a. have an active sexual relationship
b. have levels of intelligence similar to that of their spouses'
c. have grandchildren
d. a and b only
e. all of the above

4. Which of the following statements about widowhood is NOT TRUE?

a. most men widowed between age 50 and 70 remarry; most women do not.
b. widowers may be more lonely and isolated than widows, making adjustment to a spouses' death more difficult
c. older widows have a more difficult time adjusting to widowhood than do younger widows
d. most research to date on widowhood applies to older women who have had marriages with traditional gender roles
e. widows and widowers who are financially secure adjust better to widowhood

5. Which of the following is predictive of contact with friends in late adulthood?

a. same social class
b. opposite sex
c. being single
d. having children
e. none of the above

6. Which of the following statements about grandparenting is NOT TRUE?

    a. most grandparents take pleasure in the role
    b. few grandparents' feelings of satisfaction with their lives derive from their involvement with their grandchildren
    c. often people become more androgynous when they become grandparents
    d. grandchildren are closest to their grandparents in the teenage years
    e. a variety of styles of relating the grandchildren have been identified

7. Which of the following DOES NOT characterize workers who retire early?

    a. good physical and financial health
    b. poor physical and financial health
    c. dissatisfaction with work
    d. physical or psychological job stress
    e. higher than average education

8. Which of the following statements about retirement is NOT TRUE?

    a. most people today think of retirement as a just reward
    b. for most, income drops substantially with retirement
    c. the proportion of older people who are poor has risen in the last 10 years
    d. older women are more likely to live in poverty than are older men
    e. most retirees say that they want to work

9. Compared with younger workers, older workers

    a. are more likely to receive schooling and retraining to improve their job skills
    b. are as productive
    c. are absent less
    d. are more committed to their jobs
    e. are more likely to be passed over for promotion

10. Which of the following DOES NOT predict positive adjustment to retirement?

    a. being financially comfortable
    b. being healthy
    c. having considered work central to one's life
    d. having planned how to occupy oneself
    e. having retired voluntarily

11. Which of the following statements about education in late adulthood is NOT TRUE?

    a. formal education for the elderly is becoming less popular
    b. older students do as well or better than younger students in their educational endeavors
    c. older students have more problems in regular college courses, compared with special educational programs for mature adults
    d. problems of stereotyping the elderly affect their self-esteem and academic performance
    e. all of the above are true

12. Which of the following is associated with a greater likelihood of voting in old age?

    a. having more education
    b. being female
    c. being politically conservative
    d. being black
    e. none of the above

MATCHING

A. For each expenditure, use the letters below to indicate whether older adults spend more or less than younger adults.

    _____ 1. housing
    _____ 2. household functions
    _____ 3. transportation
    _____ 4. medical care
    _____ 5. personal care
    _____ 6. clothes
    _____ 7. leisure activity
    _____ 8. furniture

a. older adults spend more money than younger adults on this
b. older adults spend less money than younger adults on this

B. For each behavior, use the letters below to indicate whether men are more or less likely than women to act or feel in this way

    _____ 1. well adjusted to widowhood
    _____ 2. have close friends outside the marriage
    _____ 3. live in poverty in old age
    _____ 4. say religion has become more meaningful over time
    _____ 5. vote

a. men are more likely than women to act or feel this way
b. men are less likely than women to act or feel this way

ANSWERS TO THE SELF-TEST, CHAPTER 22

COMPLETIONS QUESTIONS

1. health; happiness with housing (p. 571)
2. more (p. 572)
3. integrity; despair (p. 572)
4. 5 (p. 573)
5. 40 (p. 574)
6. modified extended (p. 577)
7. 70 (p. 578)
8. social involvement (p. 582)
9. transportation (p. 584)
10. more (p. 585)

MULTIPLE CHOICE

1. e (p. 568)
2. a (pp. 569-570)
3. d (p. 572)
4. c (pp. 573-574)
5. a (p. 574)
6. d (pp. 575-577)
7. e (pp. 578-579)
8. c (p. 579)
9. a (pp. 579-580)
10. c (pp. 580-581)
11. a (pp. 582-583)
12. a (p. 585)

MATCHING

A.

1. a (p. 586)
2. a (p. 586)
3. b (p. 586)
4. a (p. 586)
5. b (p. 586)
6. b (p. 586)
7. b (p. 586)
8. b (p. 586)

B.

1. b (p. 573)
2. b (p. 573)
3. b (p. 579)
4. b (p. 584)
5. a (p. 585)

CHAPTER SUMMARY

This final chapter, <u>Death and dying</u>, includes discussions and
explanations of longevity, death, and the grieving process.

The section <u>Longevity</u> discusses maximum and average lifespan, and
factors influencing length of life. Longevity has been
correlated with many characteristics, including brain weight,
body size, rate of metabolism, length of prenatal development,
and age of sexual maturity. With the exception of humans,
shorter lifespans are associated with fast metabolism, brief
periods of prenatal development, and brief periods of sexual
immaturity. The <u>maximum lifespan</u> for humans, the oldest age to
which any members of a species survive, appears to be 114 years
old, and has not changed for eons. The <u>average lifespan</u>, the
average length of time that members of a species actually
survive, has been increasing for 200 years, due to improved
sanitation and medical advancements. Life expectancy, strongly
influenced by genetic and environmental factors, is longer for
females than for males, and longer for whites than for blacks.
It has been increasing since 1900.

The section <u>Death</u> discusses many aspects of death. <u>Definitions
of death</u> vary, and have become more complicated as technology
improves. Clinical death occurs when spontaneous breathing and
heartbeat end, and marks the end of life for most people. Brain
death takes place when the higher centers of the brain stop
functioning, leaving a person comatose. Cerebral death is the
death of the cortex. <u>Conditions of death</u> have also been
changing. The age of death has shifted upwards, death is more
likely to follow after a chronic illness, and is more likely to
occur in a hospital. Some people choose to die at home or in a
hospice where their choices about death are honored and death is
less expensive. <u>Attitudes toward death</u> are shaped by social and
psychological factors. Half of a sample of terminally ill adults
said that they drew strength from the support of family members
and friends. Due to changing conditions of death, people are
more disturbed today by children's deaths because they see them
as "unscheduled". Death today is considered the province of old
people. This thinking may cause people to postpone coming to
terms with their own inevitable decline and sense of loss.
<u>Developmental change in concepts of death</u> discusses how cognitive
maturity affects perceptions of death. Preoperational children
may think that death means a shrinking rather than an end to
life. Concrete operational children understand that death is an
end to life, but don't understand that it is inevitable and
universal. Terminally ill children understand death in ways
beyond healthy children their own age. Adolescents are
vulnerable to thoughts of death and suicide, but little is known
about what they understand about death. <u>Death and the sense of</u>

the future discusses how thinking about one's own life and death shifts over time. Middle aged adults think in terms of how many years they have left, and some may reorganize their lives and their time in response to this. Perceived control over the environment is a better indicator than age on feelings about the future. Fear of death is probably only present in humans, and tends to decrease over the course of adulthood. Death and the sense of the past discusses the process of understanding and reconciliation humans engage in in coming to terms with death. Erikson suggests that the final developmental task is to reconcile one's struggle against death and despair with the fulfilling sense that one's life has been meaningful. Life review, a reflection on one's past and review of memories, is a common way of achieving this. Life review may have positive or negative results, and doesn't necessarily improve adaptation ability. Stages of dying and timing of death are discussed in the section Dying. The psychological process of anticipating one's own death is made up of several emotional states. This "dying trajectory" begins when a person understands that she is dying. Most people want to know if they are dying. Kubler-Ross has theorized five stages in the dying process: denial and isolation, anger and resentment, bargaining, depression, and acceptance. This theory has received equivocal empirical support. To some extent, people can control the timing of their own death.

Grieving is a natural response to the death of a loved one. The process of grieving exerts both a psychological and a physical toll, and may be the severest psychological trauma that most people ever feel. Grief has several uses. Acute grief is traumatic, but a normal response to the loss of someone beloved. Freud suggests that grief may free one from emotional ties with the dead person. Bowlby and Parkes suggest that grief has an adaptive role, and people try to unite themselves with the dead person. Socially unacceptable behavior in grieving persons is often overlooked. There are several Stages of grieving, including shock and numbness, yearning, depression, and reorganization. Grieving for young and old may differ. People who lose an elderly parent typically feel less devastated and disrupted emotionally than people who lose a spouse or a child.

LEARNING OBJECTIVES

After you have finished studying Chapter 23 in both the text and this guide, you should be able to do the following:

1. Define maximum lifespan, average lifespan and life expectancy.

2. List the biological and environmental correlates of longevity.

3. Explain the three different definitions of death.

4. Discuss how conditions of death, including age and place of death, have changed in this century.

5. Discuss influences on attitudes toward death, and how these attitudes have shifted in the last five decades.

6. Describe the effect of cognitive maturity on conceptions of death.

7. Explain how death and the sense of the future are related.

8. Explain how death and the sense of the past are related.

9. Note how fear of death shifts during adulthood.

10. Explain Kubler-Ross' five-stage theory of coping with death.

11. Discuss the uses of grief from several perspectives.

12. Describe the stages of grieving.

13. Discuss factors affecting the intensity of people's grief.

KEY TERMS

Longevity (p. 590)

Maximum lifespan (p. 590)

Average lifespan (p. 591)

Life expectancy (p. 591)

Clinical death (p. 594)

LATE ADULTHOOD

Brain death (p. 594)

Cerebral death (p. 595)

Hospice (p. 598)

Appropriate death (p. 598)

Life review (p. 602)

Dying trajectory (p. 603)

Bereavement (p. 605)

Sudden Infant Death Syndrome (SIDS)(p. 607)

STUDY QUESTIONS

1. Describe changes in maximum lifespan, average lifespan, and life expectancy for humans in the last 200 years. (pp. 590-593)

2. Compare and contrast the various definitions of death.
    What are the advantages and disadvantages of a standardized
    criteria for death? (pp. 593-595)

3. How have changes in the age and place of death in the last
    century affected individual reactions to death?
    (pp. 596-598)

4. Chart a development progression in the understanding of
    death. (pp. 599-600)

5. Discuss the merits and possible drawbacks of life review.
    (pp. 602-603)

6. Explain Kubler-Ross' theory of stages of dying.
    (pp. 603-604)

7. Compare Freud's views of the uses of grief with those of Bowlby and Parkes. (p. 605)

8. Describe the stages of grieving. How do these compare with Kubler-Ross' stages of dying? (pp. 606-607)

9. Discuss why the death of a child might be more painful than the death of an elderly parent. (pp. 607-608)

10. Explain the differences between humans and other species in terms of correlates of longevity. (p. 590)

SELF-TEST, CHAPTER 23

COMPLETION QUESTIONS

1. Humans are probably the only species to try to push back the limits of _____, or length of life.

2. In general, the briefer the prenatal development and the briefer the period of sexual immaturity, the _____ the lifespan of a species.

3. Human children remain sexually immature and dependent on their parents for a relatively long time. This factor may explain the _____ human lifespan.

4. The maximum lifespan for humans seems to be _____ years.

5. For the last 200 years the average _____ has been increasing for humans.

6. _____ _____ refers to the average length of time a person can expect to live.

7. In 1900, the average life expectancy was _____ years; today it is about _____ years.

8. A person who reached the age of 65 in 1979 could expect to live an average of _____ years of life.

9. In 1981 in the United States the death rate among infants younger than 1 year old was lower than in 1900, and the death rate for infant boys was _____ than for infant girls.

10. The nature of the typical illness in society has changed from acute to _____.

11. As a result of medical advances, _____ percent of Americans die in a hospital, a nursing home, or other institution.

12. To avoid the degradation of dying in an institution, some people choose to die at home or in a _____.

13. Across the lifespan, people's awareness and understanding of death is consistent with their stages of _____ development.

14. Human beings probably are the only species who understand that they will die, and probably the only species who _____ death.

LATE ADULTHOOD

15. As people approach old age and death, they reflect on their past by engaging in a process called life _____ .

16. The emotional states that people experience when they face the natural prospect of death has been called the dying _____ .

17. The experience of grief and feelings of desolation that follow the death of a loved one are known as _____ .

18. John Bowlby and Murray Parkes explain the use of grief as an adaptation in which people try to _____ themselves with the dead person.

19. When infants go to sleep apparently well and never wake up, their death is attributed to _____ _____ death syndrome.

20. The death of an older husband or wife is generally experienced as less painful than the death of a _____ or of a young husband or wife.

MULTIPLE CHOICE

1. Which of the following factors does NOT appear to reduce the longevity of human beings?

   a. rate of metabolism
   b. nutrition
   c. resistance to disease
   d. size of brain and body
   e. medical advances

2. Which of the following may explain the longer lifespan of females?

   a. females resist infection and disease more effectively than males
   b. females have fewer accidents than males
   c. until they reach menopause, females have hormones that seem to protect them from heart disease
   d. fewer females smoke and suffer from alcoholism
   e. all of the above

3. Which of the following factors may explain the lower life expectancy of black people compared with white people?

   a. white people are more resistant to all forms of disease
   b. poor nutrition is more common among black people
   c. black people are more likely to live in impoverished environments with poor nutrition, sanitation, and medical care
   d. all of the above
   e. b and c only

4. When the cortex of the brain dies, the death is called:

   a. clinical death
   b. brain death
   c. cerebral death
   d. natural death
   e. none of the above

5. Which of the following factors is LEAST likely to have influenced social attitudes toward death?

   a. increasingly longer average life expectancy
   b. increase in deaths due to chronic versus acute illness
   c. the number of deaths occuring in institutions
   d. the number of old people who die from natural causes
   e. the number of unscheduled deaths in young people

6. According to Kubler-Ross, when dying people refuse to admit they are really dying, they are in a stage of:

   a. acceptance
   b. denial and isolation
   c. depression
   d. anger and resentment
   e. bargaining

7. When a person is tense, extremely aroused, restless, and in a continual search for a loved one who has died, he or she is in the stage of grieving known as:

   a. shock
   b. numbness
   c. yearning
   d. depression
   e. reorganization

LATE ADULTHOOD

MATCHING

Match the cause of death with the cohort most likely to be affecte
by that cause.

_____ 1. congenital defects from malnutrition and disease
_____ 2. suicide
_____ 3. chronic and acute diseases
_____ 4. accidents, poisons, and acute diseases

a. most likely a cause of death to infants
b. most likely a cause of death to children
c. most likely a cause of death to adolescents
d. most likely a cause of death to adults

ANSWERS TO THE SELF-TEST, CHAPTER 23

COMPLETION QUESTIONS

1. longevity (p. 590)
2. shorter (p. 590)
3. long (p. 590)
4. 114 (p. 590)
5. lifespan (p. 591)
6. life expectancy (p. 591)
7. 47, 73 (p. 591)
8. 17 (p. 592)
9. higher (p. 596)
10. chronic (p. 597)
11. 80 (p. 597)
12. hospice (p. 598)
13. cognitive (p. 600)
14. fear (p. 601)
15. review (p. 602)
16. trajectory (p. 603)
17. bereavement (p. 605)
18. reunite (p. 605)
19. sudden infant (p. 607)
20. child (p. 608)

MULTIPLE CHOICE

1. a (pp. 590-591)
2. e (p. 592)
3. e (p. 593)
4. c (p. 595)
5. d (p. 598)
6. b (p. 603)
7. c (p. 606)

MATCHING

1. a (p. 593)
2. c (p. 593)
3. d (p. 593)
4. b (p. 593)